Orchar

By the Pupils of
HALL ORCHARD C.E. SCHOOL

PRINTED & PUBLISHED BY:
WINE PRESS, 1 SILVER STREET, TAMWORTH
01827 67622

Hall Orchard C.E. Primary School
June 1997
ISBN 1 86237 041 9   £4.50

*Our children at Hall Orchard love words -
written, recited or read - and we are proud
to present this Book as a celebration of their work!
All of our children have been able to give something
of themselves to this project - their stories, poems, ideas,
pictures and thoughts. It makes it special for each
child, special to Hall Orchard and we hope that
it will be very special to you!
It is our Book of 1997 which we are sure will bring
the reader much pleasure and pleasant memories
of our children's schooldays.*

Happy reading!

Kind regards

Bob Morley
Headteacher of Hall Orchard CE Primary School

Our School

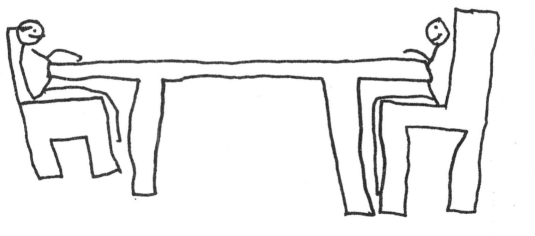

Our school

Our School has a good Headmaster
But your always being told to work faster
And at our school
There is a rule
That at ten past three
You will be free
To go home
And have your tea
And watch CBBC
on BBC
on TV

The school has a sandpit
The school has a field
But the things that I enjoy most
are the school meals

by Jamie · Clifford
Age 10

I Cannot Wait.

I cannot wait until school is out,
I cannot wait until I can be out and about.

I cannot wait until I can wear bright
coloured shorts,
I cannot wait until I can play lots of sports.

I cannot wait until the last day,
In short I cannot wait until the summer
HOLIDAYS!
                    By Adam Bradwell
                    (age eleven)

I like sports day and I like going on the field. I like going on the
bottom playground. and going to dinner with katie and emma

Rachel coyne Age 7

Our school

At my school the teachers are very Nice,
and help me with my work.
I enjoy doing handwriting most of all especially when
we design patterns.
P.E. is great I love running around, hopping on the
spot and doing short tennis.

by Isabel Blower
age 7

My Mum brings me to scool because my dad is at work
at Play time I Play football. I have Sandwiches.

Callum Peacock
Age 6

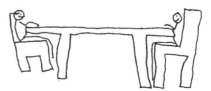

My First Day at School.

On my first day at school I felt lonely when my Mum left me. All the while I was thinking, When am I going home? I only had one friend her name was Sophie, we played in the sand pit all day long. When my Mum picked me up from school, I was really chuffed. Then I thought to mysely what will we do tomorrow?

By Lucy Graham.
Age 11.

School Days

Walking to school in the cold fresh air,
Not thinking of anything, don't really care.
Walking to the gate another day,
Working hard, working away.
I walked in the school and the teacher was there,
and she was fiddling with her short blonde hair.
There's Sam she's my mate,
Where's my friend Livy? She's going to be late.
Lucy is singing, it starts to rain
and there's Rachel she's being a pain.
Another day is finished once more,
So I return home through my own front door.

by Sophie Birkett. Age:11

Our school

At my school we do P.E. and maths among many other subjects. My best parts of maths are shape and money. I can pretend that the money is all mine!

I enjoy doing science because I like doing experiments. Short tennis is really brill. One day I shall play at Wimbledon

by mustafa

Age 8

The headmasters name is mr Murley. My favourite thing is playing on the computer. My favourite game is cat and mouse.

Jonathan Doda Age 7

Our school.

Our school is the best school. I enjoy P-E. swimming and going on trips. I love maths, especially when we do shape and make our own pictures.

by Bill Breed.

age 8

My First Day at School.

Feeling frightened, feeling sad,
Where's my mum, where's dad?
The rooms so big, I feel so small,
The ceiling is high, the chairs seem tall.
Feeling poorly, feeling sick
My mum said the day would go quick.
A white haired lady came up to me,
"Come sit on my lap," the lady said.
Her hand was warm, her smile bright
Now I think I'll be alright.
Feeling a bit better, feeling less sorrow
Wonder what we'll do tomorrow?

Samantha Felton - Betts   aged 11

our hed master is mr morley. our techer is mrs wilby and
my sister is in mrs Birdsalls clas. there is lots ov
techers. And theres a lot ov flowers. And I like doing
pichurs and learning a bout people in the past. Like queen
Elizabeth and Louis Braille and Florence Nightingale and she
was nown as the lady with the lamp. and Samuel peyps

Abbie sharman Age 7.

At school I like going into a sembly to see pupits.

zoe connell Age6

Our School
At school I play with my friends Joshua Forth
and Peter Brightman. We play throw and catch.
My favourite subject is Maths. I enjoy doing adding
and subtraction sums. I am good at this. I also enjoy
Art, particularly when we made our delicious dessert.

By Lewis Morris
Age 8

At school I like reading
and I like playing
I like going to a sembly.

Joshua Mason

Age 6

Laura plays with me

Lauren Baker Age5

Our school head master is called Mr
Morley. At school I like writing storys and
Maths. I like playing on fields. My teacher s
name is Mrs wilby. She is a year two teacher.
On Tuesday we go studio and we learn about
Elizabeth 1st and Louis Braille.

Mrs wilby

Felicity Dunn   Age 7

Adam plays
Batman
with me

Scott Widdowson Age5

our school is nice. I like school
because I get lots of hard work.
our head masters name is Mr Morley.
our teachers name is Mrs Wilby.
she is a nice teacher. We go to the
studio on Tuesday and Friday. so
far we have watched programmes about
Elizabeth I and Louis Braille.

mukti parbhoo Age 7

I like school.
I like it when we go
to whatch the vidios
in the studio.
Laura Norton Age 6

My School

My school is like a big family.
Everybody is a special person
to me. I love learning about Science
from my teacher. I like Maths and
English. I like sketching, reading
and History.
Cheryl Purvey
Age 10

ITIEOPTHEFEGSATSGL
EMILYFaCrbrother
ages5
I tidy up the things at school

MISS Chilton is my favorite teechur. She givs us interesting peesis of work and She put me with my friends. I liked the crismuss show. I played the recorder so did my friend. I am a packed lunch but wwns I hada crismuss dinner.

Emma Ross Age 6

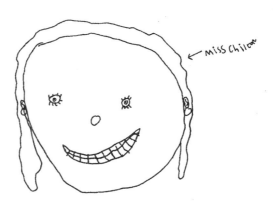

← MISS Chilton

Our School

Our School is a big school,
Its made of bricks and plaster,
It lives in Borrow-Upon-Soor,
With a wonderful Headmaster.

Our Headmaster's a wonderful man,
His name is Mr. Morley.
I like it when he's in School.
I hate it when he's poorly.

.Donna . J . Campbell.
.10 . years . old.

my favourte game is tiggy on wud.

I like gowing on the computer.
I like cooking becauser I like making thirgs.

keeley pestell age 6

<u>Our School</u>
<u>At our School</u>

If you come to our School
You will have fun
Some people will be a fool
And their work won't be done

When you are at our school
Obey this rule
Stay cool!
And at home be a fool!

Joseph Golding
9 years

I Lilk to riad Books at school.
be cos it is fun. I-Lilk to
fit Books. Icepcittat
Luch tiim. a my sowerby age5

I like to read books at school.
because it is fun. I like to
write books. I keep quiet at
lunchtime.

Our School

I really like our school. All the teachers
have helped me over the years. My
favourite subject is Maths, especially
co-ordinates. In Games I like throwing
the cricket ball. But my favourite time
of the day is going home for tea.

By Leigh Mabbutt
Age 11

Days Out

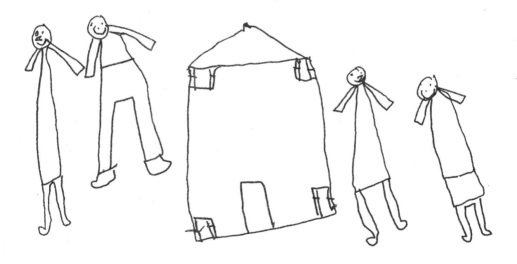

we st D at n a
and G a D

We stayed at nana
and grandad's house.

Marc Shenton

I LK gowhg on

the RodaRt

/ / Lv

I like going on
the roundabout.

Katie Brown

I wonce vere fishing with David I dyn t wabcn
The line. I didn t cache.anything then I went home

scott Bervhardi Ageb

I weht Thev wtac
Jack Breed
age5

I went to the sea-side

When i went to the sea side we went on the amusements and we won loads of
toys. When we were coming back there was water coming over the bars and lots of
people got wet so some men had to close the road down. We just got out but we didn't
get wet. When we got home I wanted to go again and my Dad said some time.

Katie sirrell Age 7

I Went to my Gramrs (grandma's)

I Playd at my Gramrs

Philip   Seaton

I my A ort Tnepoc

I am at the park.

Christopher   Dudley

I LR goig Shopig

Jade Beechey
age 5

I Wet toFr
I went to the farm

age 5
CHarLoTTe
Grant

a farm
I Went to of m
Chloe Norph
age 5

I went to the Swerte
I derde a srteerte I went
Four a wat.

I went to the seaside
I had a sweetie lolly I
went for a walk.

Charlotte Barker

This is meonabout
trip. I like bowt.

This is me on
a boat trip.
I like boats.

Joey Pickering

I Go swimming on Saturdays and my
tEachers Name is Jan and Evrey Saturday.
I Go in the Big PooL
and I was Scared of the deep bit

Emily Hartley
age 6

'I iKs wiM

I like swimming

Michael Sharp Age 5.

I went for a ride on a
white horse. It trotted and
I fell off.

Emily Golding age 8.

JAMES

I am kicking
a ball with
my dog.

Age 4.   Name: James Clifford

DaDDY and WLiLL a m MUM
ahdhr U.h.m Y ahd Me
at apih

Daddy and William
and mummy and me
at a picnic.

Bethany Jones

I Liked it in skegness because it was warm and it did not rain. I went to the fer. I liked the boats.

Harold Barker. Age 7

Illkgowigsw
imijng

I like going swimming

Daisy Hickling Age 5

Days out

The day I went to American Adventure it was great. I went on a water slide that went into the swimming pool. The food there was fantastic. I had a great time. But now we have to go home.

by Lucy Sharp

age 11

days out
I went to the pub

age 5 cheisie murray

Ietcltpc
I like the park

Libbi malohey
age 5

wen I go To wic steed
Park I go on Lots of rides
My favrt ride is The wetabix
bus michael Evison age6

we went the play uatsige och the

BIKs

Katherine Young

We went to play
outside on the bikes.

I went out to see some trains.
They wer desols and
stom trains. we went in a
coach. There wer some
electric trains. Then we
Wenthome. simon Horobin
age6

Katie

I am on the swing
My brother is on the slide.

Age 4. Name: Katie Alexander

we went to
a farm

Kate Willson

I like gowing on holieodys becas I like the things. I go fur a wuc. We go to the discow evry nit. We stay in a caravan.

Jamie Kimber. Age 6.

Wenttot ri∮e pub

We went to the pub.

Henry Wilford

My best day out was going to centre park because there was a big slide that was 20 ft tall. And I like to get fish and chip's. And I like to eat lars ou food.

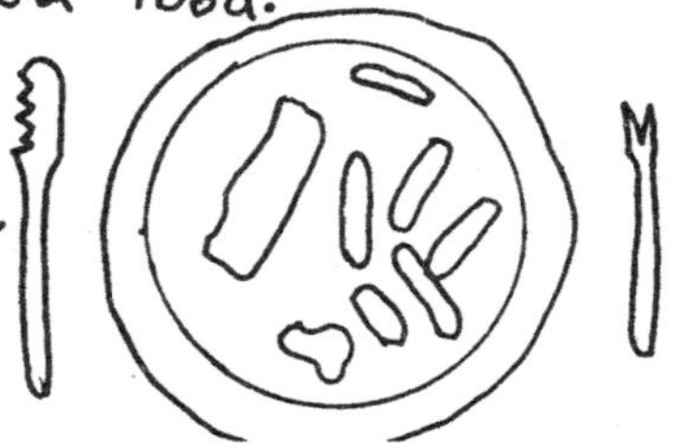

David Rhys. Age.7

Wext Wontto picnic

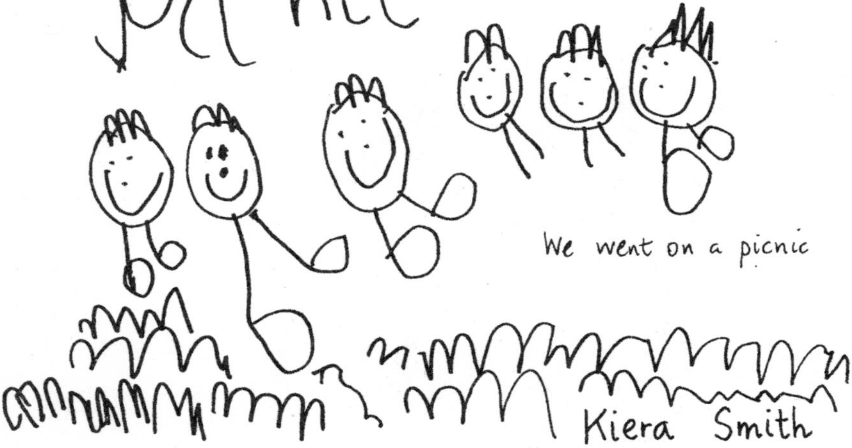

We went on a picnic

Kiera Smith

I went to Vales. There
was a Beech. My Frend
was there. We made a
sand Kasul it was big and
we cud go in it.
san shepherd   Age 6

Aston

I like to go
to the swimming
pool and dive in.

Age 4.   Name: Aston Dunlop.

Harrisonkew

I am
walking to
the park.

Age 4 Name: Harrison Kew

I like going to the
school to play with
my rowler blads of my
bike and some times my dad
pulls me dawm the hill
and thenwe go home.
Reece cunningham   Age 6

Days out

The best trip I've been on was at Discovery Zone. It's where you play on slides and climbing frames it was quite exciting. My other favourite was Snibston Discovery Park because you can do experiments like make waves and see yourself on a bicycle.

Sean Fleetwood
age 9

I went to the seaside
(I went to the seaside

Tim Hase
Lhurst
age 6

One Day I went to the zoo a lion bit my Finger off.
The zoo keeper told the Lion Off.

Daniel Wright
Age 6

Alice

I am at the
Park on the swing.

Age 4   Name: Alice Thompson

When I Went on Holiday
to center parcs
I Went in the swimming
pool evryday. I went on
This rely good snake slide.

Emma Anderson
Age 6

iwentt Osunnydo wh pork

I went to Sunnydown Park

Scott Stirk Age 5

days out

1. GO Suntimes TO
a Party afdur School
Suntimes i GO home
wev my anty
with auntie

yasmin Perry
Everett age 6

myMum went outtoafashunshw
andIWeotetothepocr

Laura Tindle Age 5

Days out

when it was my birthday, mum and
dad took my sister and I to see one
Hundred and one Dalmatians. I would
Love to have a dog like one of the
puppies. I especially liked the part where
the two dogs bit cruellas bottom! The
next day I had a party
with a dinosaur cake!
by Scott Maloney age 8.

IW ESETFROGSU
ATTUMThemseuM

I went to see
the frogs at
the museum

Samuel Ward   Age 5

uPmrcYD
h Potfu
U+mY
Nua
fouly
Luvv
Weg fuht

±OFz

I went swimming
one day
I liked
the floats
the best

kellyMartin
age 6

I have a set of shells
I brought them From the sea.

I have a set of
shells. I brought them
from the sea.

Madeleine Smith

I Go to my Nana and GrandPas to Sleep the night
and in the Morning I went to swimming and I
swmd and I got a bachr and it was my 10th.
Metr bachr and when my Nana told my mum and was
varry Happy that I ve got a bachr and my Dad
was Allsirtd and he Give me a big
hug and he kissd me and On next Friday I am going
to my Anty Minos house to sleep the nigt and
my Ubael Andy will by me some sweets

Eleanor Dunn
age 6

I Wish

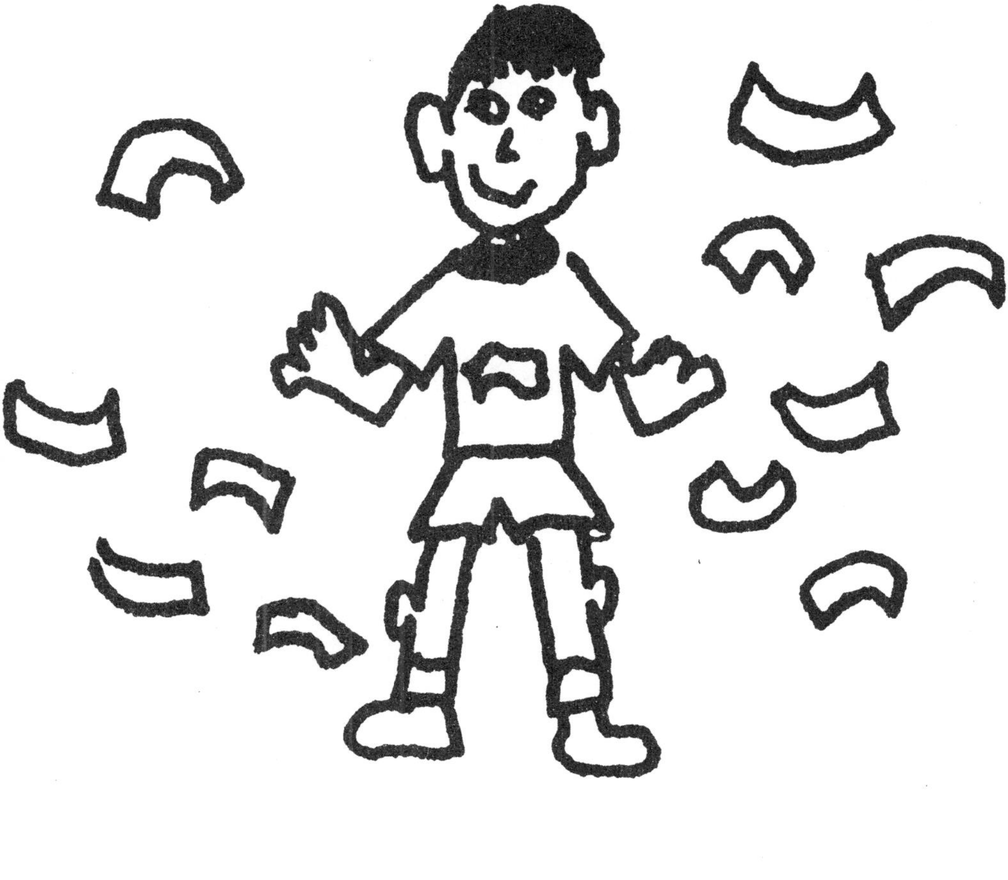

I wish, I wish.

I was watching T.V. It was basketball
and Bulls and Magic were playing.
Magic were winning in the first period,
it was 28 - 17 to Magic. I wish that I
could play basketball for Magic. I wish
I could go into the T.V. and play basketball.
I would score a basket. It would be a dunk,
and we would win 78 - 70 !

By Chris. Squires.   Age 10.

I wish I cud biy a cwis queen

Samantha
LAUNDY
age 6

I wish I was super star
football is my game
playing for the best
Fowler is my name.

Liverpool is my team
And the fan's would sing
"Fowler you are our dream
you are a football king!"

by Dane Bingham
age 10

I WISH

I wish I was a Vet so that I help all the injured animals and give them
back to their families. You get paid lots of money and have lots of
laughs. But it can be sad at times when animals are too badly injured
and die.

Victoria Hughes

I Wish

Name William Fuller
age 8
yere 4

I wish to be a Formula 1 driver, to drive in a William Renault.

I Wish

I wish I was a professional darts player.
Eric Bristow is my favourite player.
I cannot play darts at the moment because
my darts are broken and my dart board
has gone mouldy. My second favourite
darts player is John Lowe. My darts are
John Lowe darts. My highest score on
darts board is one hundred and seventy
four. My dad is the best. He can get one
hundred and eighty. I should be getting some
Eric Bristow darts for my birthday.

Nick Gardner   Age 11

Wishes.

I wish I was a cartoonist because
I like making people happy and
making them laugh. I'm a part-
time comedian as well. Hey-what
about this as a joke? what
stands in the middle of paris? 'r'
get it? My teacher is very good at
drawing. So is my Mum. I havn't
seen dad draw yet. made ya look?

Imogen Webb
age 8

_ I wish I was......

I wish I was a footballer and played for Manchester United.
I would play in Central Defence and might even play in
Midfield. If I was chosen to play for England I would like
to play at Right Midfield. It would be brilliant if I scored.
It would be even better if we won the World Cup. If I
was Captain I would make sure the opposite side did not
score by organising the defence.

By Richard Conway Age 10

I wish I went to The pub.
And I played on the snooker
table and I wun the cup.

Thomas Burton . Age 6

I wish

I wish I was an actress doing all those films.
I wish I was a teacher telling people off.
I wish I was in River Dance doing all those steps.
But then again Just be yourself, or so people tell me.

Ellen Upton age 10

I wish to be a truce drive be cus my dad is a truce drive

irly waet to be a truce drive

I really want to be
                a truck driver   michael   age 6
                                   clifford

I Wish

    I   Wish   I   won the   lottery, so   I   could buy
a Ferrari and   a   new   house. I Wish you could never
run out of   money.

Nick. Allen   Age 8.

I Wish

I Wish I could play in the National Basketball
Association, I Would play for the Chicago Bulls.
I would be their leading Scorer and get 30 baskets
in every game. I Wish I could play along side
michael Jordon. Every time the ball bounces I Would
See him putting the ball in the basket.

by Liam Richards
Age 11

I wish.

One day I wished I had a horse and a week later my wish came true.
What was amazing was I did not get one I got one hundred.
That was what was amazing and some of them had foals.
So in the end I had one hundred and fifty five.

By Kirsty Gould
Age 11.

I wish

I wish one day I could become a famous
Show jumper. I would take my horse to the
big shows, like Olympia and Burleigh.
I would do the course and get a
clear round. Then I would do the jump
off and get a rosette.

By
Emma Hodges

Age 11

I wish

I wish I had a MacLaren Formula One road car, but they cost over half a million pounds. I am a little short of, £634,350 infact. But if I win the lottery, I might manage it! The only trouble is, it has not any room for luggage and has only one seat. I dream of driving top speed down a clear motorway with no coppers to give me a speeding fine.

Jamie Anderson

Age 11

I Wіh To be I F0O t bᴄh
E LІК F00 t ᵴo mᴄhІ Wот F00т
тad Mɣ ɴaɴ

I wish to be a footballer
I like football so much I watch football round my Nan's.

Thomas.Lofthouse

age 6

I wish

I wish I could play for man. unt

And beat West Ham. 3-0.

by David Buxton Age 8

I Wish

I wish I was a Spice Girl and sang on stage.
I wish I was Emma but I also would like to be
Geri. I know all their songs off by heart. My
favourite is, Who do you think you are?.

My best friends are April, Jenny and
Kathryn.

By Jessica Wilson
Age 8

I wish

I wish I was a pilot.
Flying planes across the lands and seas.
See birds flying in the air.
Taking passengers to New York
on Concorde in midair.
Landing at airports with a big bump.
Flying over a 10000 feet high.
Looking down like a giant so big.

by
David chan age 8.

I Wish

I wish I played for Coventry City F.C. playing in left midfield.

Name. Mark. J. Dipple.
age. 9.

I Wish I Could.

I wish I could go to Australia and sit on the golden sands.
I want to cuddle a koala and jump like a kangaroo.
I may even walk like a Platypus.
    My dream would be to see the sun go down at
Ayers Rock.

By Joanna Boyes.
                    Age 11.

I wish

I was a girl who did not have to
got school and I wish I could lay in bed
all day long. And only do a bit of work a week.
I would like to live in a big house, with
sexvants.

Age 9
Tarren dark
by
Tarren.

I Wish

I Wish I could fly high in the sky.
I Wish I could jump very very high.
I Wish I could run very fast.
I Wish I could be good at football.
I Wish I could Live for ever.
I Wish I could be very strong.
I Wish I could be a basketball player.

Anthony Whitbread Age 11

I Wish

Playing for United is my dream,
I do not want to be like East 17.
I'd be good at hosting Shooting Stars,
I also want expensive cars.
I'd love to lie out on a sandy beach,
Writing a postcard and eating a peach.
Having a great time under the sun
Back soon your loving son.

By.
Gareth Williamson
Age 11

I wish I
had a tree house.

Age 4. Name: Morgan Bywater

I wish

I wish I could go to Sweden,
to see my best friend Hannah Beddet.
She has been my best friend ever since we first met
in mrs morrison's class
Hannah came to see me at Easter.
We went to the wacky warehouse. After we had been
to the wacky warehouse Hannah slept at my house.

by Georgina lockwood

age 8

iwiwDhdfmih
I wish I was a fireman
Ahdrew Chapman
agg 6

I Wish
I wish I could play at Wembley in the F.A. Cup Final.
I would be the captain and score in the last minute
and win the cup for Chelsea. I would lift up the cup
and you would hear the crowd roar miles away.
I wish I could play in the NBA for the Seattle
Supersonics along side one of the greatest
guard in the NBA . The Supersonics would win the
playoffs.
My greatest wish is that everybody was as
fortunate as me and there were no wars and no one
would suffer.

By Chris Clarke
Age 11

I Wish
I wish I could go to Manchester United
and play for them in depence and play with Palister,
G. Nevel and P. Nevel. My best player is David
Beckham.

Name Adam Caren
age 9

J A M E S

I wish I could see my Grandad.

Age 4. Name: James Reed.

I wish

I wish ~~there~~ were such things as dragons
I'd get one as a pet.
~~Although~~ I'd have ~~to take~~ it back
If it burnt the TV set.

I'd ~~take it~~ with me to school
And ~~feed~~ it on the ~~book~~ of rules.
~~Although~~ my teacher would object
And make me and dragon both upset....

So the dragon would eat her too
And then spit out a bone or two.
And all the pupils would say "Cool!"
And escape from school down to the zoo.

James Taylor
9 years.

I wish

I wish that could win the lottery and
have a ginormous Mansion. I would
roll in money and go to lots of parties

Author: Marc Grant
Age ten

I Wish

I wish I could play for Leicester City in the Coca Cola
Cup final. I would like to score the winning goal in the
last minute of extra time. What a moment that would be.
Then I would lift the shining trophy high in the air and
listen to the noise. All I could see would be blue, white
and yellow.

By Leigh Gray
Age 11

I wish the world was covered ih chofolate.

I wishI could Silly in thesk i yI wishI wasequeen

Kerry Sharp age 6

I Wish I can everpit

Age 5   Katherine Harris

I wish

I Wish I was a
Super Star footballer
running down the wing
and Scoring Lots of
Super goals. I would
cross high balls in,
taking corners and
throw-ins too. Playing at
wembley I would score
the winning goal.

by Stuart Burton - Blythe
Age 10

Ashley Sutton
As
ages

I wish I had a snake

I wish I could live nere the
beach because I could go to the
beach when I want to. I could sun bathe
all day long. I can eat ice cream and
I can go to the pair.
Rachael Smith Age 7

I wish Sammy Morton
To be u age 6
DOG

I wish

I wish I was a basket baller
Dunking in the nets
Dodging all the players
And keeping girls for pets.

I wish i was a footballer
Scoring all the time
I'd like to end my poem now
but I cannot make it rhyme

by: Ben clifford
Age: 10

I wish.

I wish I could play for Man United.
And play against Leicester City. I wish No one
Lived on the streets.

Tom chamberlain. Age a.

I wish I had a horse becos
I can rid it. I can feed it.
and I can stroc it.

Laura Young age7

My wish came true

I was watching T.V. It was Football.
Man U were playing Leics and Man U were winning
3.0. Then I was playing in the match
and I scored my hat trick and
then I wock up. I was dreaming.

by Thomas Dixon

age 10

I wish I was a
Soldt
Ryan wright
age5

I wish I was
a soldier.

i wiSH iwoS
a PriNSS

Age 5 Georgina white

I Wish

I Wish I was a whale
with a big blue tail.

I Wish I was a frog
sitting on the log.

I Wish I was a snake
slithering by the lake.

I wish I Was a cat
sitting on the mat.

by Nathan Morris
Aged 10.

I wish I was a dog to
jump on top of pepl

Joshua Thomas

age 5

I wish

I wish I was older.
I wish I was strong
and that I did nothing wrong.
I wish I had all the money in the world.
I wish I could buy my mum every pearl.

James Rook

10 years

I wish I had a nuw kite
bcus it is brocun
I wil pley wiv my kite

Michael sturgess
age 5

I wish

I wish I was a footballer.
I wish I was a star.
I wish I played for Leicester.
And travel very far.

I wish I was a footballer.
I wish I was a star.
I wish I played for England.
And score the winning goal!

Kyle Flinders
9 years

Magicians

I wish I was a magician, making people amazed with what I can do. Reading peoples minds, telling them the card thats theirs - three of hearts! And sawing Simon Newton in half. I wish I was like Dominic on CBBC. I wish I could do all his tricks so people will be even more amazed, especially my mum, dad grandma and grandpa. I really love magic and I want to be a magician when I'm older

By Ben Wilson age 8½

I Wish

I Wish I Was a football Star.
and playing for manchester united.
maybe I could play as a Striker
and Score a lot of goals.

by Tom Aston

Age 9

I wish I had a beby
bcuz I can pic him up

Natalie Allen
age 5

I wish!
I wish I was a footy star,
and be a goal keeper.
And maybe score a goal or two,
and always shine like new.

By Ben Preston
Age 9

I Wish! I Could .....

I Wish I could go to Australia to
see my best Freind Peter Fairburn.
To play in his Swimming Pool and
run around in the play ground and Find
some crystals in the mud. And catch the
Spider but I dont Want to go near
the red backs there the most poisonous in the
world. Edward Tansey age7

I Wish.

I wish I was a basketball player.
or a star for Newcastle united.
I wish I went to Paris and Australia.
I wish for New house.
I wish for an alsation dog.
I wish I was a life guard.
I wish I was an a plane.
I wish I saw a Rocket.
I wish I was in a Rocket Zooming
into Space.

Ashley Hodgess

9 years

I wish I had guinea Pig
   Bcus I Love guinea pigs
I Love them so so much
Jennifer cross age 6

        I wish.

That   no animals or humans beings suffer when
they   are ill, and that   there   are   no weapons in
the   world.

Flora   Sherwin
Age 9

   I wish I cud go to evry singl
   FootBall   match that the foxs
   PLAY

   stephen canning
   age 5

I Wish

I wish I was at the Queen's palace because
she is 75 years old! I would count all
of her money for her. She has got millions!
She might give me a hundred pounds. I would
buy computers for my school and new P.E. things.
I would give the rest to poor people. I wish ......
It would come true. Leon Smith Age. 8

I wish I had a house made of sweets
and at night time I would have
a sweet. It would be a bit like a
witchis house and it would have
candy floss on the roof. It would be
pink and green.
Carly Gay Age 7.

I Wish I had a Parrot

they went awa to
Hevn

caLLUm GoLding
ages

I wish

I wish I played for Liverpool. I wish they would win the league.
If I did play for Liverpool I would play in goal. My favourite player
is Steve Mcmanaman. My favourite goal keeper is David Seaman.

by Daniel Gay

Age 8

I Want my toth to
cm at cus I Want
to hav a peny

Kirah Garton
age 6

I Wish I was a funny man.

I wish I was a funny man. I would make people laugh. I would say to them "I can't help laughing I know whats coming next." And I would do some magic and amaze people infront of their very eyes. What a great choise of words don't you think? For my next trick I will make a spoon jump in a glass! Amazing!

by Timothy Bell
age 8

I wish I was a princess I wud like the juwuls and her prity dress. I wud be wunderful and the best in the howl wuld. Every one likes a princess.

JULie Harrison Age 7

I wish

I wish I could fly high and through the clouds.
Watch the birds and planes fly.
To watch the people on the ground.
And see birdseye views of everything.
To watch people scuttling about on the ground like an ant.

by Lee Hands. 10 years.

I Wish
I wish that there was no school
and then puff, I was in my house.
I wished two more times.
I wished one more time
but it did not work .
By Ben Croft age 10.

I wish
I wish to live forever.
I wish to have tentousand wishes.
I wish to win the lottery.
I wish I could drive.
I wish I had a basketball.
I wish I was a footballer.
I wish I was a star.
I wish I could fly.
I wish I was a bird.
I wish I was a dog.
                Chris nabbutt
                9 years.

I Wish

I wish I was a cat, so I could climb the wall's

and climb the trees and go on adventures and fight other cat's.

Sit on the sofa and be fussed by all my owners

and stay In all Night. In the morning I would go out the cat flap and

teach a young cat How too fight, and make new Friend's too.

in the winter I would call my friend's. we will go on adventure's

together and go Back Home to get warm.

by Hannah
Forrester
age 8.

I wish at I had
anyw RYT SO I
can FlY

I wish that I had a new
kite so I can fly.
Samuel Roberts
age 5

when I grow up I wish that
I could play for Leicestercity.
Football club.
My very favourite player is
Hesry, but I also like Steve walsh.

By Ben purvey

Age 7

I WISH

I wish there was no school,
I wish I could play pool
I wish I was more cool
I wish I had a swimming pool
I wish I had a car
That would go very far.

Adam Widdowson

I Wish

I Wish I was invisible so no one could see me coming.
I wish I was a bird soaring and sweeping up up in the sky.
An Eagle, a pelican or maybe just a magpie.

by Rachael Budd age 11 years

I wish I was a comedy Star

The curtain would go up,
I would go up too!
A cheer and laughter!
I love this reaction. "We have
a man at the back. He makes
his own gravy. The count of monty
Bisto!" The audience go wild —

they love me to bits. What a
great feeling. I'm on top of the
world. Better not look down!

Nick Copson
age 8½

I wish

I wish that I could go on a trip to
Frace. When I have been to France
before I enjoyed travelling on the
ferry. and camping. I would really
love to go to EuroDisney near Paris.
and spend days going on all the
exciting rides. my favourite ride
is the roller-coaster. I love the
sudden lurch as you go down
to the bottom really fast.

By Peter Brightman
Age 7

I wish it was christmas becusI like geting toys and I get excited. Jonathan Graham age 6

I Wish

I wish I could fly,
like the birds in the sky.
I wish I had a million pounds,
so I could buy, lots of hounds.
I wish I didn't have to come to school,
all I would do is play football.

by Daniel Blower
age 10

I wish for a
ntbc
motorbike.

Luke Pervin
age 5

I Wish....

I Wish I Was a millionaire!
So I could go on Holliday's to a place like France and go on
Adventures. I Would Spand money for the poor and
charities.

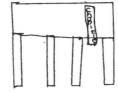

by Nicola
cross

age 8
class Mr Allen

one day I would put 100£ pounds in a charities Tin
enough money for the poor to get clothes

The End

I wish I could .....

I wish I could do everything like make
computers and draw everthing and make
foot balls. I am really good at foot ball and not
good at Golf. my best sport is basket ball
I wish I had a real good nets like oliver.
I wish I could have some goaly gloves too.
and I wish I had lots of money. then I could go every
Where I Like. I could go to a basket ball
match.

by Jonny Palmer age 8½

I Wish

I wish I was a Foot ball star scoring lots
of goals and running up and down the pitch.
I would love to hear the crowd chanting my name.
perhaps one day I will play for manchester
united

By

Adam Towell

Age 9

I wish for a majic
wond to wav it

Faith

Porter

age 6

I wish I had a dog. I wish I had a Slave.
I wish I had a moon. I wish I had a Palace.
I wish I had a hole bag of sweets.
I wish I was a SPICE Girl.
I wish I had a summer dress.

Ellie Pickering. Age 7

I wish my mummy and daddy wud win the lottery. They wud win 5000 pounds and they wud give Me all That I wonted.

Amelia Cummins. Age 6.

I WiSh I Could....

I Wish I could be a comedy star. I could do Millions of magic tricks. I'd cut Nick Copson in half and I wobld only Stick him back together as long as he would promise to behave! I would probaby feel very funny. My reaction would be like a show off you could say.

by simon Dawson.
age 7 years

I wish for a bag of money
and I wish for a cat
a I wish for Jure rae
jewellery
Ashleigh Sharman
age 6

<u>I Wish</u>
I wish to become a sportsman and to play for the
English Cricket Team against Australia at the Oval.
I dream of scoring 154 runs and taking 7 wickets
that would probably help the team win for once.......
I hope!

By Andrew Exley   Age 11

<u>I WISh</u>   Louise Durston ,

I wish I had a MILLioN PouDs IN cash.
I Wish I was Rich and I lived in
a big house and had lots of clothes.

I wish my sisdar was nis to me.
I wish I wish was I a ryul football
playar. I wish was I was a grown up. I wish
I was an artist. I wish I was a
teach ar.

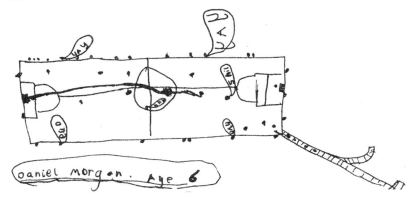

Daniel Morgan. Age 6

I wish

I wish I could goto Di sney
Land to See Donald Dack and I
could goon the rides. I would
take three friends. They are Leon
and Ryan and Jonny. It would be
great.

name. Oliver Faulkes age 8

I Wish

I wish I had a Black horse. It's name would be Black Beauty. I would make it a stable out of wood. It would live in a field. I would go to see it every day. I would feed it and ride it round the street

by melissa Betts age 8.

I wish it was my birthday be cus I can opn my present wot I want is a polly pocit.
Lucy Stephens age 5

I wish.....

I wish I was a shopkeeper and work on the till all day because you press buttons all day. You get lots of money and I don't want my shop to be robbed...So...its going to be a bread shop! Because I mean why would anybody want to rob a bread shop?

by kit sfy Heald age 7

I wish I had a hamster.
I wish I could have lots of chocolate.
I wish I could go horse riding.
I wish I could fly.
I wish I was a Princess.
I wish I had a Play room.
I wish it was my Birthday evrey day.
I wish I had a baby sister.

Nicola Dale age 7

I WISH I could......

I wish I was the boss of Disney Land.
I want to be the boss of Disney Land
because then I could watch the
videos, read the books and cuddle
the toys. I could invent new rides
for the people to go on. They would
be even faster and scairier. I would
let poor people come for
free!

By Ryan* Barker*

age 8 ½ years

I wish I wuos Riah gigs

Ryan Gigs because

I Wont to scow gowsfotmy

score goals

Mum and dad

I Wish

I wish that I could have a C.D player,
So that I could play my favourite artists.
I Like Boyzone and Spice Girls best.
I could have it on very loud.It Would
really annoy my sister.
                    by   Sarah   Whitmore
                         age   7

iwShicBCOtSeSiD

I wish I could go to the seaside

mattKWHeWeSageo

I wish I could swim with a killer wale all my life. I wish I could be a better recorder player. I wish I could beat my Daddy at football. I wish my little brother would be kinder. I wish

Lauren Emma Bowler. Age 6.

I wish

I wish that I will learn all of the english words.
I wish I could go back to Hong-Kong.
I wish I could have a big house.
I wish I didn't have to go to school.
I wish I could fly.
I wish I didn't have to do P.E.
I wish it was Summer.
I wish my room was a bit bigger.
I wish I was rich.
I wish I would never die.

Eva Wong
11 years old

I wish for a baby sister
I wish for a tree house
and play in it every day
I wish for Long hair

Sophie Godfrey McKee
age 6

I wish

I wish I could be a racing driver when I
grow up. My favourite racing driver is Damon Hill
the current world champion. He drives for the
Arrows team. I wish that there was a race
track in New york and that I could win the
cup. That would be the best prize ever.

Edward perry
age 8

I Wish.

I have always wished that I could
be a filmstar. My favourite filmstar
is sylvester stallone. He is very good at
acting I like him better than any other
filmstar ever. Sylvester stallone is very
powerful and muscly. Whenever I play
a game I pretend to be him.

by Ayden smith.
Age 8.

I wish I was a millionaire.

I wish I was a millionaire. I would star in all the action films. I'd marry someone rich and famous and then we would buy a very big house. I'd shop all day and swim all night.

But that is in the future I've got ten more year's to go. I guess my wish will have to wait.

By Emma mansfield
age 11.

Keep smiling

I wish

I wish I could receive a lot of presents.
I wish I could happy everyday.
I wish I can see my sister every day.
I wish I be good everyday.
I wish my goldfish will never die.
I wish I could go to swimming every day.
I wish I could have the Spice Girl tape.
I wish I can have the quiet time to reading every day.
I wish I could have a dog in my house.
I wish my english will better.

Cathy Kwok
10 years old

I wish

I wish I could be a cat.
Climbing up the trees.
peering at people.
Washing my self before I go to sleep.
playing with balls of wool.
Chasing mice at night.
being stroked by people.

by Becky Rogers

Age 10

I Vish I could play football. And beat ervyone. in the World
I would help Lester city win evry one. Me and Walsh Would
team up. And walsh and me would score all the goals.

Matthew
Perret age 7

I Wish.

I Wish that I was an adult.
I Would like to be thirty years
old and a teacher. I Would
like to teach year six and
have thirty four children in
my class. At school I enjoy
Maths and Handwriting. I especially
like adding up, counting and using
a calculater.
By Sam Lucas age 7.

I wish

I wish up on a little star shining and twinkling bright.

I wish up on a flying bird making strange sounds in the night,

I wish up on a coat of shining armour so I could win a strange fight.

I wish up on a shining car so I could ride it when it is light,

I wish upon a puppy which I hope won't bite.

I wish up on an aircraft black and white,

I've came to the end and I think you will like it. I hope you might.

Louise Bailey
age 10

I Wish

I really want to play for Leeds United Football team.
I just sit there all day and dream.
I know other people who would too.
I guess Barrow juniors will just have to do.

By

Edward Coyne

Age 10

I wish I was a..........

I wish I was a footballer playing for Newcastle United (the best team in the world), I would have thousands of pounds pouring in every week! I would buy a personal limousine, a mansion, my own racehorse and a personal jet. Then I would become the captain of England and guide them to become World Champions. Then Newcastle would win the League, the F.A. Cup, the Coca Cola Cup and the Champions League. I wish!

By John Petrie Age 10

I would like to wish that Colin Cooper came out of my wardrobe. and I wish I had good shots and good scil. I wish I playde for forest and we wun evre time.

Matthew Brodwell
age 7.

I wish.

I wish I could go to Newcastle to meet Newcastle Utd. So I can see them play a match. I wish I could meet them and get their autographs. I would go to the shop at the stadium. I wish I could have a tour round the stadium.

by Paul Cochrane   aged 10

I Wish

I wish my birthday would never end
So I could get a lot of presents all the
time.
I wish I could go to Disneyland to be
with Minnie mouse.
I wish I could have a dog so I
could play with it every Day.
I wish I won the lottery so I could
buy a great big house.

Zoe chan
9 years

I wish I was a Millionaire.

I wish I was a millionaire. I would be a stage
performer in all the acts and shows. I would marry someone
famous and swim around all day. I would go to all of the
fashionable shops with my purse and pockets bulging.
But that is in the future. No one knows what will happen
to me. I hope my wish comes true.
By Sarah Golder
Age 11.

I Wish

Pollution, pollution, What is your Solution?
Pollution, pollution, What is your Solution?
Dropping litter everywhere
What is happening to the air?
Pollution!
I Wish there was no pollution

Alex clarke

age : 8

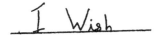

I Wish

I wish there were no wars and hunger.
No bombs and third worlds at that.
No people without water and that is that!

Name Hayley Warren

Age 9

I wish I had a . . . .

"I wish I had a dog" I said to my Mum but she did not listen because
I have asked her about six times. It will be my birthday tomorrow
and my Mum and Dad said I might be abled to have a dog. It was
my birthday and I was really excited. I wonder if my Mum and Dad
have got me a dog because they have not come down yet. It was
in the afternoon when they came down with a box in there hands I
opened it "Yes yes" It was a puppy Labrador THANK YOU.

by Craig Brooks Age 10

I Wish.

I wish I was a shooting star to fly high in the sky.
I wish that I was imortal so I would never die.
I wish that I was an adult so I did'nt have to go to School.
I wish that I was as rich as ever to buy a swimming pool.
I wish I was a famous singer to sing out loud and clear.
I wish I was a powerful witch to make my sister disappear!

by capri clark

10 years

I wish

I wish I could fly in the blue sky
And go right up in the blue sky
I wish I could fly ——— High.
High ——— High ———
High

by Sam Hickling
9 years

I Wish.

I Wish I played for Leicester because I am a Leicester Fan!
I play for Rothley I am top Scorer I have got twenty two goals
this Season. And If I did play for Leicester I Would want to
play upfront. My Best players for Leicester are Kasey Keller and
Garry Parker.

Stephen Chapman (Age 8.)

Luke Dipple age 5

I WiSh To BeY a fuTBuL PLaY
football
anO PLay f rurcov unTreY SiTeY
coventry city

I Wish.

I Wish i played for Liverpool and played
up front with Robbie Fowler and scored goals and Set
up players So they can Score goals.

By
Tom John Brooks
age 9

I Wish

I Wish I could have a go-Kart Then I Can have races
With my friend.

I Wish I could have a SKateboard
then I can skate down the hill.

I Wish I could have a Computer then I could
play on it all day.

age 9   name Joe Lee

My I wish poem

I wish I was black belt in Karate.
I wish I had a giant party.
I wish I could go to the moon.
I wish I had a golden spoon.
I wish I had the biggest room.
I wish I had a smaller brother.
I wish I had some hubba bubba.
But most of all I wish that I could run
at the speed of light.

by: Patrick Taylor   age:8

<u>I Wish.</u>

I Wish I could play for Man.United and
I Wish there was no robbers.

LEWIS Bowman. age 9

<u>I Wish</u>

I wish I were an aeroplane so I can
fly in the sky.

I wish I were a fish so I can
swim in a bowl.

I wish I were a super star so I can
sing a song.

Gemma peacock
Age 8

I wish

I wish I was Bruce Lee,
Cuts and bruises on my knee.
Jumping around on the film set,
I'll beat that bloke in, don't you fret.
I'm seven belts away from black,
but that's not enough to break a back.
Darren my instructor's pretty cool,
He could easily break a wooden stool.

by Jon Page
age 10

I wish

I wish I was a basket ball player.
I wish I could do a Slam dunk.
I wish I was a super star.
And play for chicago Bulls.

Ben Horn
Age 10.

I wish

I wish, I could have a horse
to look after and to take care of.
It would give me something
to do.

by Sarah Hemsworth

I wish:

I wish I was a Snake.

by Jamie Snow. Age 9

Special People

Special People

I always have a special person every single day.
I used to have an imaginary friend called Snowy.
Sometimes my best is mrs Bradford other days my Mum or
Dad. But all the time I have extra special friends like Rosie
and Hannah who have moved away, of course I always have
Georgina, Peter, Lucy, Jennifer and Natasha.

By Frances Bywater 8 yrs

Special people

My special person is Mrs Cant because she helps
me with my work.
Is I do some thing wrong then Mrs Cant helps me to
get it right. My favourite subject is Maths.
Some times I get it wrong but then I get it right.
I like doing work alot. but my special person is
Mrs Cant.

Smile

ACE

by Zoe Dale
Age 9

Special People

My Mum and Dad are the most special people
in the world. They look after me day and night.
They give me food and keep me warm. My Mum
and Dad are the best. They take me to many places,
but my favourite is the cinema.

By Karl Fleetwood
Age 11

Special People

My grandma is a great friend to me,
If I hurt my leg, my elbow or knee.
She's never too busy to play or talk,
And sometimes we even go on a walk.
In the car she makes up quizzes
If she sees a cow she really wizzes
She always thinks of others before herself.
And does not have alot of wealth
But I do not care,
No matter where
I will always love my grandma.

Tom Butler age 10.

Special people

My special people are called
Simon Grayson, Stevey Stevey, Claridge, Emile
Heskey and plus Kacey. There my special
people because Simon Grayson scored the goal
that made City win on the away goal rule.
Emile Heskey for making us draw at Wembley.
Stevey Stevey. Claridge for scoring the very
important winner at Hillsborough. But Last
Kacey Keller for doing lots of important
saves.

Tom Norris   age 9.

A Special Person

My mum is a special person.
Her name is Karen.
She does a lot of things for me.
She is a very special person.

She does the washing, the ironing,
She cleans our bedrooms because they are
tips!

I can't imagine life without her!

Chloe McGuirk
10 years

Special people

I have two special people called Jennifer
and Joanna. Jennifer is my best friend,
but I play with both of them. We play tig
and twister. When my dad was small
Joanna's uncle played with him.

by Josephine Lee

Age: 8

Special People.

My Special friends are...

Sam is funny and thinks I'm an android (weird!)
And helps me when I'm down and is always around.
My other friends are...

Tom is very mad and silly.
Other than that he's extraordinary.
My other friends are Adrian, Kyle and Jamie.

By Joe Hall.
aged 10

Special people

I like Arsenal, Rik Mayal's Great!
Michael Jordan's cool, Liam's my best mate.
I like L.A Lakers, they're really cool,
I like David Seamen, but I hate Liverpool!
I love Gillian Anderson, she's really great,
My brother chris is cool, Vinnie Jones I hate.
I like Geri and Van Exel is brill.
Clare my sis is wicked and I don't like Damon Hill.
But Mum and Dad I love you best   You're a
really fantastic pair.
Keep the world and all the rest
ITs for you I really care!

        Andy Clarke   Age 11

        Special people.

When I pick up my teddy I'm sad. It reminds me of a special
person. My teddy was made by her when I was born. It reminds
me of the past. My family were sad when we got that phone call
from the hospital on that Saturday morning. It all happened five years ago.

            by Chris
            Caukwell age 11

My mum is speshel to me because she cares for me.
She cooks the tea. She makes me feel better when
I am sad or upset. She buys me football stickers.
She helps me do things. She gives me somthing to
eat when I want it. Im glad shes my mum

Craig Bull Age 7

God is so big and spesl.
He is in Hevn. He awes.
Pals for us.

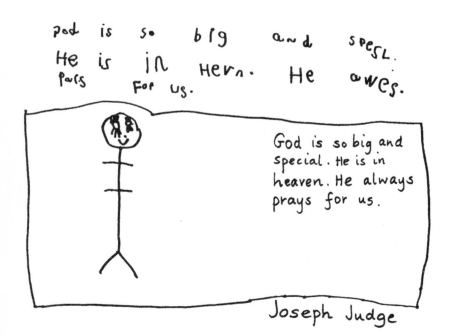

God is so big and
special. He is in
heaven. He always
prays for us.

Joseph Judge

Nanna is see sh uu sh uu weeyz
luucaftame wen my mummy is
at wac

Nana is special.
She always looks
after me when my
mummy is at work.

Lauren Palmer   Age 5

my Dad is Special because he takes me to good places. He buys me sweets.
He takes me to foot ball traning. He takes me to Coventy es ground. He looks after me.
He dose my reading with me. He teaches me cricket. me and Dad have fights. my Dad is silly and
He makes me laugh. my Dad is the best.

Adam Dipple   Age 7

my   mum   is   in
America
Richard Greenhough 5.   Age

A 2C 4 W

This is my
special friend
my mummy

Age 4. Name: Andrew Devine

My nana is special because she buys me football stikers.
When i'm not feeling well she makes me better.
She buys me sweets.
She lets me use her bingo dobbers.
She gives me big scoops of ice cream.
I love her

Sam North age 7

Imogen

This is a
special person
the headmaster

Age 4. Name Imogen Garton

chloe murray
Age 7. SPeShel PeoPle

My family is very,
SPeShel to me. And I take
care, of my brother and sister too.
And I take care of my family too.
dale daniel dad mum   mitchel
                    Jacob   chelsie

CHrIStopher

My special friend is my daddy.

Age 4. Name: Christopher Horobin

Speshle people. peter Schmeichel is a speshle person because he is a good goal ceaper. Eric cantana is a good player he has scored for us. Ryan Giggs is good at skills.

Sam Thomasson age 7

natalie

I am with my best friend my mummy.

Age 4. Name: Natalie Kwok

SPeShel Peole

MY grandad is SPeShel bee
cos hee didnt get hurt in
the War but my grandma is ill.
And my uncle nearly got shot but he
is ocay.
Elli Mae Age7

Jonthnshape

This is my
special person
my daddy.

Age 4. Name: Jonathon Snape

SPECIAL PEOPLE
Grace is my BEST frend
I Play wi th her in the
Pla grand and I Play
horses andI Play sairis
to gether
age 6
Abbie ELPhick

mrEAImSle F̶O̶U̶LKLK

My Mummy likes me

Beatrice Kimber Age 5

special   people   Le Lp   us wen we go

roy   my futtr   Psnw Is a Puleslades
They   heelp Pecple   hw goroy Rachael
                                    McMillan
special people help us when we go   age 6
wrong my favourite person is a
                            policeman
they help people who go wrong

my dad is sspecial
and he tecsme
tothe sm
        farm.

Tom Mills
age 6

I wish   I   could   see
my   cusun   in   Australia.
He   stayed   at   my   house
he is called   Rodney.   he is
very   nice   to   me   he
is   very   very   sreshul.
He   went   back   to   Australia
on   the   aeroplane.
olivia   Ellis - Thorne   age 6 years old.

I Like Eddie he takes us To the
Wacky Warehouse house after school some Times. He gives
us 50p after school Too. Eddie is very spesnul To me.
Lawrence Bywater Age 6

special people help people
And pules lades help us whenwe
hav a buget come to ar howes
     burglar   house
                    Gemma Crate
                       age 6

police lady

Cantona is a famys
foot ball pLayer he
pLays far man united
he is french.
Adam cLifford Age 6

I luv my daddy
Tyler Buswell
age 6

SPECIAL FRIENDS.

My mum and dad are the best, they keep
me warm and feed me well .I love them loads.
My dad always lets me go with him at weekends
on his motorbike, we go for miles together. We go
camping in the summer holidays too. They are the
best mum and dad ever .I would not swop them
for anything in the world.

Matt Seaton age 11.

My special uncle is called Barry.
He has got three dogs. He has got 1600
lambs. He has a big house but he has
got a swimming pool. I like him. He
has a jacoosy and it's hot and I went
in it

Sophie Burton Blythe Age 7

Special People

My brother Jonathan
Has autism you see,
He does not understand
Things, as do you and me.
He really likes to play
And run round with a ball.
He does not like to run and
Skip, he does not like many
Sports at all.

My brother Jonathan
Has autism you see,
He can still be friendly
To my family.
We all love my brother
Even though he can be
Trouble,we all think he is
Really great, with a tendency
To turn things to rubble.

My brother Jonathan
Has autism you see,
Although he is rather
Strong, stronger than
You or me. He is really
Great, he brings us lots
Of joy. We all think he is
Really good, that little
Autistic boy.

Chris Martin
Age 11

Misertpusagz
Jiz

Beh Lucas age 6

my favourite person is
Jesus

Special People

My mum and dad are very special to me.
Without them I would be very lonely and sad.
I have some other special people and they are my friends.
However, they are not as special as my Mum and Dad.

By Lee Thomas
Age 11

Special people.

My name is Stacey Chilton I am 9 years old.

My special people are my foster mum and dad because they love me and care for me alot. They take me out to the pictures and macdonalds and buy My things. My foster mum's daughter's look after me too.

by

Stacey Chilton

9 years old.

Special people

My nana was very
speial to me because
she was very ill.
She had something called
Altzheimers which is a very
bad disease and it took her
away from me. I only got to
see her about once or twice.
She was very special to me I
think about her every night.
I sometimes cried about her
because I missed her so much.

by Elise Barlow.
Aged 10 years.

Special Days

wen it is July it will be my berfday. wen it is
krismas I will be eksited. wen it is easter I
will be eksited and I will eat some egg.

Matthew Taylor. Age 6.

My Special day

My special day was when
I got my rabbit. My rabbit was
called Bunny. Bunny was black.
One day Bunny died and I
was so sad. Now I have got two
rabbits called Thumper and Snowy.

by Katy Shaw

Age 9

I had a special day at my cousinshouse.
I went to the seeside. At theseeside I
walked in the water.

Sean Greenhough Age 6

My Special Night

It all happened last night. Wednesday, 17th April, 1997.
Leicester City won the Coca Cola Cup final at Hillsborough.
The score was one nil to Leicester City against
Middlesborough. Steve Claridge scored the winning goal
in the second half of extra time. It was a really special night.

By Shaun Seaton
Age 11

I lik my brthday bcs I can
hava bousy casl

Alexandra Copson age 5

i LPLa Ye P i Post he
PtL

I like playing pass the parcel

Lauren Robbins Age 5

My special day.
My special day was when my
baby brother was born, because I
was the first to hold him. Lots
of people came to visit us in the
hospital. His name is Reece and
he is now thirteen months old.
I can no longer hold him as he
is too big.

By Sophie Townend.
Age 10.

one day I went to a wedding. I wor a soot. It was red, I looked cool. Daniel Moore Age 7

Special Days
One of my special days was my last birthday when I was seven. My Mum and Dad took me to Beacon Hill in the car. Grandma and Grandad came from Derby to be with me. They gave me a bag with Harrods on it. That was a lovely present, whilst my cake was a pink PIG!

Hannah McKay
Still age 7!

On Halloween day I like going out and I like going into houses and I like scareing people olote. At summer time I like it a lot because it is my birthday.

Matthew caren. age 6.

Speical Day's

One speical day I was getting Ready for School because I am going after Schod to a Party and I am going at 8.00.

by Emma Filley Age 8

Special Days

The present Sat before me. Unopened, bright red and green Christmas wrapping paper dazzled my eyes. My fingers trembled as I quickly unwrapped the wrapping paper on the parcel. Could it be? Would it be the present I always dreamed of?
It was .....!

By Alex Allen
Age 11

When it's christmas I want
to open all my presents all at
wons I am so happey I think
I hav lots of presents.
    Hannah Taylor
        age 5

My Dad has a new house. I like visiting and Picking blackberries in His
Jaden. I'm lucky to have two houses.

                            Charlotte Theobald Age 7

                    Special days
My Special day was when I bought My
dog called Jordan. He is three years old
and he's a black Labrador. He sleeps
indoors. At Six O'clock on Saturday morning
My dad takes him for a walk to old
    John in Bradgate park.
                    by Steven Ballard

                age:- 10

My Special Day

I remember walking on to the stage for the first time. I heard the music start and all of a sudden I had really bad butterflies. I started my dance and I looked in to the audience, I saw my Mum she was beaming from ear to ear and I felt better. When I had finished the applause was satisfying. The judge seemed to take hours, but it was worth the wait. I had one of the best days of my life. I came first and I was awarded a gold medal, my friend Sophie came second. In fact, I enjoyed it so much, I enter competitions every year.

By Olivia Fines
age 11

Special Days

In the distance I can hear,
Wedding bells ringing clear.
Gold and Silver wedding bells,
Ringing aloud that tells.
Everyone far or near
"A wedding is here!"

Joy is found when they say "I do!"
And "I love you"
Spending their lives together
And no one could stop them, whether
They're Queen or King,
After the lady has the ring!

Katherine Willan
9 years of age

Bonfire night

It's bonfire night.
The fire is bright.
Tonight's the night the sky is alight.
The fire crackles.
The fireworks pop.
Out comes the food it's stinking hot.
5ᵗʰ of November.
Do you know what it means?
Sausages, potatoes, bangers and beans!

Amy Harding
9 years

I lac my birthdays because I lac my
birthday presents. I lac Christmas. I lac
Christmas presents.

Sam Boyes. Age 5.

My most special day was when we bought
Tangle my boat. She is 30 foot long and 10 foot
wide. She can sleep 7 people. The fastest she
can go is 10 miles per hour. She was built
in 1967. The marina that she stays in is
called Hermitage Marina. The best place I've
ever been to on Tangle is Noble's field which
is in St. Ives which is in Cambridgeshire.

Emily Nash
Age 9.

iamgoingto
myweding

I am going to my wedding

Age 5 Jodie Hartley

My favourite day is my Birthday. Because you get
lots of presents. My Birthday is in April. my best
party was when I was 6 years old Because I was alowd
lots of people round. my mum made a cake with a
horses head on it.

Sally the oldnam
Age 7

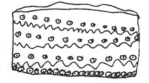

My special days

My special days were when my little sister was born and when my cousins came to visit me. I had never seen them before because they live in Australia. My other special days were when I got my first bike and when I won a SeaLife competition on holiday in Weymouth.

by charlotte wilson
Age 10

Special days.

PGL.
On Monday the 17th of March, year six went on an Adventure holiday. We did lots of activities, such as raft building. I pushed lots of people in the water when we were raft building. Our raft was the best of course, and we saw a comet that night.
The assault course was wicked and Lucy fell into Gazza's arms.
The disco was very loud but fantastic. The house was Victorian and spooky. It was the best holiday I have ever been on.

Lauralea Smith

Special Days

I like special days. One was when my mum organised a disco day in our back garden for peter and myself and some freinds. she played all our favourite music. Beavers took me to the Leicester city football ground, where we watched city play astonvilla this was Very special because it was my first match and Leicester won!

James Conway
age 7

Special days

My first day at school was really scary.
I had a teacher called Mrs. Morrison
She was really nice and friendly.
We had to paint a picture of someone really special to us.
I drew my mum and dad.
I made a friend called Liam he sat next to me.
It wasn't scary any more. I had loads of friends
and its really fun.
"Mum - can I go back and do it all again please?"

by Matthew Harrison.
Age 11.

my Favourite day is christmas day.
because I like the decra shens.
And I like the presents. And I
like the angel at the top.

Lauren Hemsworth. Age 6.

A Special Day for me

A Special day for me was when Jerry my hamster died
We buried him in the garden and let him sleep in
Heaven. I'll always remember you Jerry and I'll still
pray for you.

Charlotte Page
9 years.

I WOT To go w in the hs aT
Wollaton Hall

I want to go in
the house at
Wollaton Hall.

Annabel Dargie

Special Days   Katie Litherland 9

I am going some where special to day and I
am going after school, and I hate wear a fancy dress.
I am going to where Baw peep has lost her sheep and I
am going to come back at 8:00.

zantabrismeprests

Santa brings me presents

Age 5   Nichola Newton

Special Days.

Tomorrow is Dressing Up Day for Book Week.
What shall I wear?
What shall I be?
I go to my Mum I need a Character before
tomorrow.
What shall I be?
I know! Mini the Minx.
All I need now is a costume.
I get all tarted up
But then I get to school and what do I find?
A load of Dennis the Menaces.

by Sarah A Chamberlain.
Age 11.

Animals

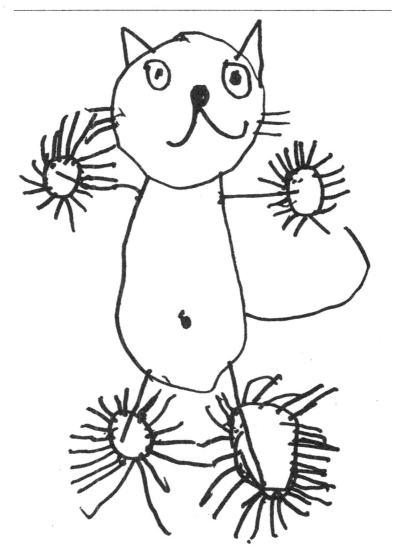

Wild Animals   Animals

The parrot is a colour full bird.
Some of the colours are red green
and blue on the parrot. Parrots fly
very high in the air. Parrots have
preditors like dogs and lions.
Parrots make lots of noises.
Parrots like eating seeds.

           Michael young.

ML bds cam on mi
Sholder
        christeopher Beadle
age 6

Animals

I have one rabbit called Beau. His birthday is on the 15th August. He is a lovely rabbit and he means alot to me.

My favourite animals are dolphins. I love seeing them jump above the water. I love the colour they are, as well.

by
Rebecca
Anderson Age:9

Animals

My favourite animal is an aardvark because they have long tongues to lick up ants. The thing I like best about aardvarks is their long noses. I think that baby aardvarks are really cute. If I had an aardvark I would call it Alfred. For his exercise I would take him on really long walks.

By Peter Exley age 8 yrs

Animals

My hamster is called Geri.
She's a female.
She's ginger with white patches.
She's 6 weeks old.
She loves to climb.
She hates to come out
but after 10 seconds she loves it!

By Kathy Harriman age 9.

Animals

I wish my gerbil had not died.
He was called, "Jimmy the gerbil."
He was very special and ran
round and round his cage. He made
me laugh. one day I would like another
gerbil.

by Serena Broughton

Age 9

animals

m]cat Is Funy

She was caching

FLies Lasdhle

Grace Elsmore
age 5

Animals.

If you were an animal what would you be?
I can think of lots of animals including me.
Cats, dogs, rats, mice,
some animals can be nice.
snakes, alligators, lizards, crocodiles,
These are all reptiles.
What would you be?
I would just like to be me.

By Rosie fuller age 11.

Animals.

My cat is good He Paws me When he's on the Settee. He Bites my toe nails. I give him a scratch on the tummy.

Christopher Snape.

age 8.

Animals
My pets are all small except for Pip
he is very tall. I have got a hamster
called Snowflake he loves a bit of cake.
I have got seven rabbits too, Sooty,
Snowy, Sandy, Patch, Shadow,
Poppy and fat Floppy. They are
all very special to me.
Dean Sutton
Age 11

My Pet

I have a cat his name is Elvis.
Elvis has sharp claws and black and white
fur. Sometimes I play with Elvis and he lays
down.

by Luke
Clarke
Age 9

Penguins

Penguins are loving and gentle
So kind and innocent.
They are black and white with yellow beaks.
They waddle around all day.
They swim in the sea and catch fish.
My sister loves them as well.

by Lyndsey Bakewell
Age 11

Gabby

This is
my favourite
animal a cat.

Age 4. Name: Gabrielle Maxfield.

My favorite animal is a hamster because i have got one
and i love it very much. it is brown and white. Evry night
he gose on his wheel and makes a terable noise. I dont Pick
him up very much Because he Bites.

Thomas Doherty Age 7

Our dog Sally
is the baby of our family.
She sits on the chair
barking away
then has to sleep
for the rest of the day.

by Rachel Baker

Age 11

My favourite animal is a cat because my. cat is cuddley and I play wiht my cat. My cat is black and brown and his name is Speedey

CharlotteMontague Age6

Animals

I love my rabbit every day
I would hate it if he ran away.
His name is loppy
His ears are floppy.
When I go to school
He looks really cool.
When people go past his cage
He stares to go in to a rage.

by
Harry attenborough
age9

I LeiQo aNiMals

AdaMRiLeg
age6

Animals

My hamster eats it's dinner,
though it's always getting thinner.
When it's tummy rumbles,
It never never stumbles.

When it drinks it's water.
It's teeth will start to slaughter.
When it's in the sawdust,
It will make a fuss.

by Geoffrey Aylett
Age 9

Animals.

I like cats because they are friendly and
playful. They purr when you are friendly to them
and at night they come and sleep with you. I've got
6 cats. My favourite is my black cat called Black
he sleeps with me at night. He purrs when I stroke him.
He is sleepy and he is five years old. He does not
like dogs.

By Zoë Beachey   9 years old

Animals

I love all animals. My best is the zoo animals.
I like monkeys the best in the zoo because
they make me laugh. They fight and squabble
all the time. They are very funny and fun.
They jump in trees all the time and eat
bananas all the time too.

Natasha Sutton
Age 7

Animals

My cat sits at home on my knee,
If it was a lion it would eat up me.
I have to make my cat's dinner
But if it was wild it would be a winner.
My cat purrs when it goes to sleep on the floor
But if it was wild it would probably roar.

by Nicholas Hartley   Age 9

octopos goo

I like dogs

Ross Allen

Lions

Lions are cute, soft and fierce.
They are not very friendly.
They wake up at night and go to sleep at dawn.
They sleep all day but sometimes wake up.
They eat any kind of meat.
They eat antelope, wild cattle and other animals

By paul Hudson age 10

I love my lamb

Anna Claydon

Animals

My poem

The birds were singing in the trees.

The Fox walked along the grass.

The Squirrel climbed up the tree.

The cloud turn into pictures in the Sky.

The flowers bloom with smell.

The Leaves change colour with the Seasons.

The Sun goes down.

By Eleanor
Marlow

n. Tnemonkeybym
< EE

The monkey bit my Lee.

Sam Robinson

One day There was a Mummy
bird. It had a baby
chick. When It gruw up. It
flid with its Mummy to see
the werld.

Tasha Grant Age 7

chelsea

My favourite
animal is a
cat

Age 4. Name: Chelsea Cato

Animals

My favourite animal is a dog.
I have got one myself. Her
name is Misty. She is grey. She
fetches the toy when you say
fetch but she won't give you it
back. She eats our food but not
Chocolate. My dog has really soft
ears. She has got brown eyes.

By Lucy Barber.
age 8.

Animals

My favourite animal is a hamster. Apple and
sunflower seeds are my hamster's favourite food.
A hamster's natural habitat is in the wild. Hamsters
like fresh water to drink. My Hamster
has a ball to sleep in. Hamsters
are Ace.

By Abigail Whitlock

Age 9

My Pets

I have got six horses called Widge, Cocoa, Rusty, Frosty, Brand and
Tea. I have got six dogs called Chelsea, Mint, Nellie, Dotty, Nepper
and Toby. I have got nine cats called Walter, Tuppy, Sid, Mampus,
Tom and four kittens. I live on a farm, we have got two hundred
sheep and fifty cows. Sometimes it's like Noah's Ark!

By Sam Young
Age 10

Animals

Animals animals fish, dogs and cats.
Mice, rabbits, guinea-pigs and rats.
I love animals because they're so sweet.
Some are so scruffy and some are so neat.

Animals can be short or long.
Some can be weak and others strong.
Some can live in the jungle and some can live in the sea.
Some can live on land like you and me.

Katie Farmer

9 Years.

I wish I could have a cat.

Name: Alexander Gunningham
Age 4.

Animals

My favourite animal is a tiger. I Love to read about them. I'd play With one if I Saw one, I'd play With it all day. A tigers food is meat It's the largest and most powerful cat. They live in India and other parts of ASia. There are no tigers in Aƒica a tiger has beautiful dark stripes and I thin they are cuddly.

By Natasha Craig
aged 8.

t tgs glot me

tigers growl
at me

Natasha Buswell Age 5

Animals

I have got a dog She is called Snoopy.
mum and dad had her before I
Was born as She is Now ninetech.
In dog years that is one hundred
and twenty Seven! I Love Snoopy very
much. She is black and White and is
a Jack Russell terrier. Her Birthday
is in August.

by Joshua Forth
age 7.

ILKEMCESBEXLEHCLMSKES

I like monkeys because they climb trees

Lauren Breed Age 5

Animals.

my   favourite   animals   are   pigs, because
They   make   funny   noises   and   snuffle
around. This   is   because   Their noses
are a funny   shape which I Love.
I would   play   with   Them all
day   long   if   They   were my
pets.   Every   day   I   would
feed   them   on   grass   and   pig
food.
        by
        Kayleigh   Gray   age 8.

A l h s i W !
z o o

I wish I had a zoo

Age 5   Maxwell Cummins

Animals

My favourite animal is a dog.
I have a dog called Sam, who cuddles me.
He is brown, white and black and sits
when I say sit.
Sam barks when people come to the door
and I love him lots.

                    by   Gemma   age 8
                          Flanagan

ILiK h a scbecushecmsdntojy
plysWithme

I like hamsters because she comes down
to play with me

Age 5   Leonni Etchells

Animals

I have a dog. His name is Buster. I play Ball
with him. He is a real tackler. He is The best
friend I have ever had. When I wasn't born
Buster used To sleep in dad's slipper. Lucy
says he is her dog But I think he is
mine. I say to Lucy you have your own
dogs and cats. I take Buster for walks with
Jessica my Best friend.

April Vanns
age 8.

<u>Animals</u>

A   poacher   in   the   woods   one   day,
Sees   a   tiger   and   runs   away.
Dives   in   the   river,
finds   with   a   shiver,
the   crocodiles   are   hungry   today!

Timothy   Hart
10 years

Cameron

This is my
favourite caterpillar

Age 4. Name: Cameron Spence

Animals

I love animals, they are just like humans. But
you can tell secrets to animals and you will
know that they will not tell anybody.
I know it sounds silly but my pet Guinea
pig knows all my secrets.

Eve Desjardins
age 11.

my dog eats cat food
She is funny her
name is milly. She
Jumps up.
                    Lauren Age 6
            BOWman

Animal's

my Dad said to me "do you want to go
out for the day?" and I said "where?" Dad said "come
to the zoo with me. and help clean the animal's." I asked
"can I have a look around as well?" "yes" you can, you can
look around first and then clean the animal's with me." My
Dad said to "me what is your fravourite animal's?" A babby
donkey and then it's a puppy." Dad said let's get going. So
we got in the car and went to the zoo. When, we got there
I looked at a lion. Lions are very firce but this one was a
sleep. There were two lions. Then I looked at the pig's. They had
a flat nose and a curly tail and one rolled in muddy
puddle and it smelled. Then we saw all the other animal's
and then I helped clean the animals out. It is hard
work looking after animal's.

    Sara maw
    age 8

my fish eats
fish food and
He Swims a

rad and a rad
he likes his Stans.

Kelly Tipping Age 6

Horses

I Love horses. I like to watch them jumping
and galloping. I like Riding horses and grooming them.
I like jumping them. I like helping peaple that work at the
Stables. I like going in the field. I like going on Hacks. I like
watching there mains flap about in the wind. If you
go round the back of a pony they might buck you.
If you go round a ponys bottom when there are
flies about then you might get hit by their
tail, it might hurt. This is what ponys or horses
have to wear when peaple ride them, a saddle, a

Bridle and the Bit on the Bridle and the neck-
strap and the numbner.

By Ana-Maria Moore
Age 8

The elephant has a long
trunk and has big ears
and it has a nastey smell
Tomos Pritonard age 6

Animals.

One moring I got up and went on my
farm and I went to see the horses
and they have got a tail. Then I
whent to the cow's and They have a
tail We have got some Duck's and
they haid a little pond. The duck's
have a libble beak and They can
fly and the horses eat carrots.
Then I went to the bird's and I
fed Them as well. Then I went in
my house and I Went to bed.
    the End.

age 8 Name katie
years morgan

My pet cat is called Pepsi and its favourit game is head butting. And if you put a Chicken nibble under her nose She picks it up in her teeth and then drops it again because it's to big For her mouth. pepsi is black with sharp teeth and brown eyes With a pink tong and sharp claws on her paws. Pepsi is a fierce cat and Frighters other cats out of our garden by chaising them. And at night she comes into my bedroom and Lies down on my bed as well. Nicholas Anderson age 7

Animals

I saw a pig on a farm. It was a fat pig. It had a curly tail and a thin nose. It rolled in some mud. It liked playing in the mud, and it had to have a bath.

It went in the mud again! We had to put it in the bath again and when we had bathed it we put it in the cage. It had some babies. They were tiny baby pigs I got to hold a baby pig. And we got to see some sheep. They all had baby sheep. They had wool on them. It was good fun watching all of them playing. We went on a tractor to take some straw to the barn. We went to see some ducks. The ducks paddled in the stream. We threw some bread for the ducks.

Sammy Beechy age 8 year

I like my rabbit because it is a baby one.

I like my rabbit because it is a happy one.

I like my rabbit because it is black and white.

I like my rabbit because I got it foh my bir th day so

I like my rabbit because it belongs to me.

Alistair Cochrane. Age 7.

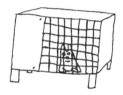

i am happy with my

kitten

Age 5 Hannah Jarvis

On munderI found a hejog. It was hongry
I gave it sum milk. Hey dranK all ov it.It
dranR uP evrer bit ov it. I Was suPrisd.I Skfl
atmy rantsand my grandadshouse.

Bill. Handler
Age7

Animals

One morning I was in bed and I just remebered
I'm having a visit to the farm today with grandad.
Then I lept out of bed and grandad was
waiting downstairs. I jumped into the car and I
was singing: "We're going to the farm, farm, farm,!
Granddad you've got your wellies on and I've
got my slippers on! " I stepped in a muddy puddle.
My slippers were full of mud and when I stepped in
the puddle it went sqwelch. by Lauren Anderson
Age 8 years.

I want to swim with
the dofins.I Lic dofins
becus theyplay trics. I
Lic dofins because itcan
balans ballson itsnos.

Lance MAnsfield Age6.

Animals

I Love aniamals and when I grow up
I want to be in the R.S.P.C.A
I want to be in the R.S.P.C.A because
I want to make animals better. some
animals are in danger and I want to help them too.
My most favrite animal is a dog because
they are soft and my second favorde is a bunny
rabbit and i love puppyes too. They are very, very
cute. I want a dog but mum dosn't want one.
me and my sister and dad want one. But my house isin't
big enough even for a giny pig.

8 years old Sian Allen

Animals

One day there was a rabbit called Rubbish and a mole called Nosey.
Rubbish was 2 years old and Nosey was 1. They had lots of adventures
together, so here is one of them. One day Rubbish and Nosey went for a
walk together, suddenly they heard some rumbling, so they went towards the sound.
The ground was starting to get hot but Rubbish and Nosey could not feel it,
suddenly they fell down a hole. It was an earth quake. There was fire down there
and they both died because it was too hot. That was their last adventure.

The End

By Felicity Hurst
Age 9

my favourite animal is a dog. his name
is Hector. He is a Labdur. He is a blac
Labdur. He has pedigree pet fud. He is 11.

Fiona Thurston Age 8.

Pet Animals.

one day I got a rabbit and it was black
and Brown and white and he was called Bob.
I have got two cats, Rosie and cracker. Rosie is the
oldest. Then one day Bob ran away. mum and Dad
said he had gone so I went to see. Then I saw
that he had ran away so I went to my bed
room and cryed. I hope he comes Back.

bob my Rabbit

Rosie my cat

cracker my cat

Katie Smith
8 ½

Animals

I have got a hamster it's name is max.
He eats sunflower seeds to his hearts content.
He runs around his wheel very fast indeed.
He will do anything to get out.

He is always getting out. We find him
here and there and everywhere. He runs up
the stairs in 20 seconds. He is a
CHAMPION.

by James Adamson.

Age 11

My Pets

I have two rats, two gerbils and one dog. The rats names are Arnie and the other Dolf. The gerbils names are Toffee and Snowy. The dog's name is Ben. We have had the dog for along time. He is a lovely dog. We have had the rats for about a year and the gerbils for about two years. We had a cat but sadly he died. His name was Bear and he was sweet. I love animals and if they are hurt I try to help them.

by Carly Sharp   age 10

I luv ridin my pony

Bethany Hodges age 6

The Tiger

The Tiger is my favourite animal.
They have black spots on them.
So they are good for disguise in the long grass in Africa So they can catch there predators. They eat meat.

By Tom Neal
Age 9

Animals

One day I woke up and I went
Down stairs and I saw my grandad and
Grandmar and they asked me if I wanted to go to
the Zoo I said " oh yes please. Dad I'm going
to the Zoo. " I saw a lion, a tiger, puppies, Birds, Pigs
and I saw lots of other animals too. I enjoyed my Day
with the animals.
Name Amy Breed.
age 7 and a Half.

Dogs House
5 Dogs
Bark
Bark

ⁱLKf ɛ

I like fish

Age 5   Thomas Peacock

Animals

One day I went to a pet shop and I saw
Lots of animals and the animals there were a
rabbit, bird and puppies, kittens hamsters, Ginny pigs,
Chickens, hens, Penguins Fishes in a bowl, rats and ducks. But
my favourite of all was the Big black Spider hanging on the
wall!   Name: Amy gould
                    age: 7 and a Half.

Animals

D is for dogs I like them a lot.

O is for oh my dog eats so much.

g is for I have got a dog called poppy

S is for sad my dog is sad when we leave
                                    the house.

                    By Gemma Norton
                    age 10

I went to the Farm and I saw the animals and I saw the horses and the ostriches and then I went to see the lion at the zoo. I had a good day at the zoo. I told all my friends and my friends said wicked! Adam Aston . 8 years old

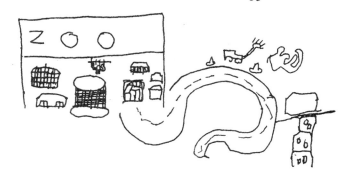

<u>Animals in the sea</u>

Animals in the sea.
Animals in the sea
Dolphins, whales and porpoises.
Animals in the sea.

Animals in the sea.
Animals in the sea.
Starfish, sealions and tropical fish.
Animals in the sea.

By Lucy Bryan
age 9

Animals

The bug

My favourite bug is the stag beetle. It grabs little bugs and eats them.

The cat

I like the cat, its cute and furry. They can see in the dark and jump over walls. You keep them as pets.

dog

The Hamster

The hamster sleeps in the day and is awake in the night. You keep them as pets too.

Jonny   Adamson
age 8

iLCELE **gaf**S

I like giraffes

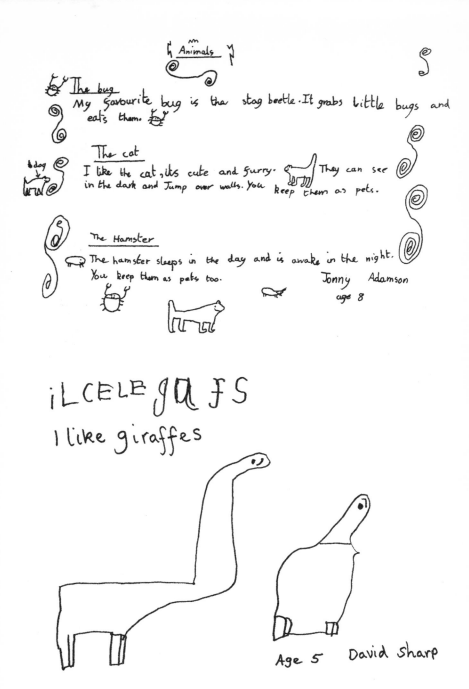

Age 5   David sharp

I hav a dog and to cats.
christopher THEObaLd
age 5

ILCSLC I like seals
EmiLY Jane
kew
age 6

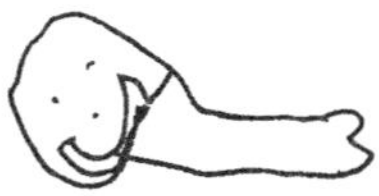

My Animals

I have two horses and a cat and one dog called Jasper.
My horses are very big and some times I ride them.
My dog is Very lovely he is black. My cat is called Billy he plays a lot and he brings mice back to the house he is to years old.

by Angela Mcwilliam
year six

Animals

My hamster is called Speedy. He goes to sleep in the morning, then he wakes up at night and goes on his wheel.

Aimee Blower 8

Animals

Some are big and Some are small,
Some are short and Some are tall.
Some are thin and Some are fat,
Some are spooky like a bat.

Some can run and some can walk,
Some can whistle, Some can talk.
Some can sink and Some can swim,
Some can balance on their chin.

Dogs and Cats and Kangaroos,
Many more are at the zoo.
Rats and Cats and grizzly bear,
Tigers, Lions stand and stare.

Monkeys swinging from tree to tree,
Spinning around so easily.
Look out for rare animals in the zoo,
their lives are threatened by me and you.

by Melanie Cornish 9 years old

Animals

Animals are big and small,
Short, fat and very tall.
Rabbits and frogs bouncing,
Tigers and lions pouncing.
Fish are swimming in the rivers,
Bats seem to give me the shivers.

My favourite animals have to be,
Rabbits, guinea-pigs or a pony just for me!
A pony trotting around the school,
A rabbit acting very cool.
Guinea-pigs being very loud,
and sounding very proud.

Charlotte Perret
10 years

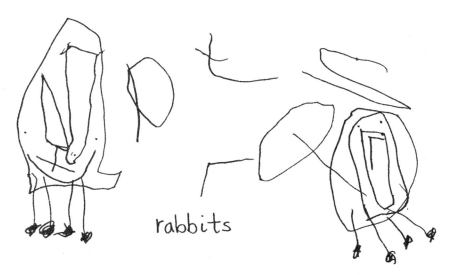

rabbits

Liam Wallis Age 5

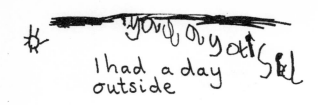

I had a day
outside

Age 5
Heather Whittington

Squigalo

1. A long time ago,
   There was an animal called Squigalo
   Squigalo was short and fat,
   Squigalo looked like a rat.

2. When dinosaurs died out,
   Squigalo survived.
   He ate a plant called lilyrot,
   But that poor plant soon died.

3. So Squigalo burried into the earth
   And slept for ten million years,
   He woke up in a forest
   And had four hundred fears.

4. First he met a rabbit,
   Which turned and ran away.
   Then he met a giant cow
   But then he ran away!

   Adrian Bull 10 years

5. Squigalo didn't know what to do,
   He tried to kill himself.
   Then he found a magic potion
   He drank it all and with a BANG:
   He was swimming in an ocean!

I wish I had the hamster

I wish I had
a hamster

Emma Wilson Age 5

My pets

I Love my dogs.
They play ball with me.
My dogs' names are called Toby and Micky.
I have a cat called speedy Ganzarely.
But we call him speedy.
Speedy plays with me every day.
He plays ball with me.
I Love my cat and dogs.

Nigel Montague   age 9½

My Best Dog.

My favourite animal!!

My favourite animal is a cat. They are fluffy and they are fat. Thats why my favourite animal is a cat. And I like that :!

Jessica Bailey
age 9.

OLiVerPage
age 5

I WISh COde hav a cat

Animals

I like animals because you can have them as pets. I have a dog. And you can see animals at the zoo like elephants, lions, snakes and turtles. Some times you can go to Sealife centres in Birmingham.

Age 9
Jack Billing.

by
Jack

Animals

I have a pet animal It is just my pet.
She is a hamster her name is Daisy.
I like to get her out of her cage.
She walks all over my bed.
Sometimes I put her in
her ball. At night she
makes a noise on her
wheel. I clean her
out every Saturday
so she does
not smell.
by charlotte Ellis
Age 9

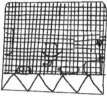

ILC@LeFANt SCOSINEVRODAN
CLCSANt

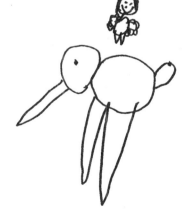

I like elephants
cos I never rode
an elephant

Age 5   chelsea Longstaff

Animals

I love receiving a new pet. First
I got a rabbit and we
called it Fluffy. Sadly it died
from a stroke. She was a
really cute girl. Now, I have got
a hamster called Rocky and two
guinea-pigs called Bubble and
Squeak.

Age: 10

by Jim Moore

I like my dogs becus won bites and
the other doesn't bite and I play wif
the wun that bites. I play wif the won that
bites becus it chases after me.

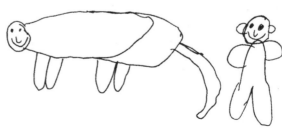

carrie-anne Neal Age 7.

Animals

I like cats because they are friendly cuddly
and furry. I've got a cat her name is pusspuss
She is Playful & Sleepful. She sleeps on beds
chairs and other places. One day She came through
the Window.

by Rebecca Howells Age 9½

my dog Tabby is cyut
She is Blac and WIT
She is Wondeful
She is sML
AprilBetts a geo

I like horses

Millie Neal Age 5

My Pet.

I have a kitten called Casandra. She is severn months old. Casandra is very playful. She likes sleeping on my mum's chair. My mum has a doll on her chair and Casandra cuddles up to it. We call Casandra Casey for short.

By Georgina Lockton. Age 8½

Stick Insects.

I have some Stick Insects eggs they are in a tank. I cannot wait for them to hatch out. They are really weird creatures swerving in the wind. Eating privet leaves and staring out at the world. I cannot wait to clean them out.

by
Tom Eldrich
Aged 11.

I LiYc aniMaLIS blcos They.
are fury and bicos som are nis
               because
and som are bad thats wy I liYc.   nice
               because
aniMaLLis Thomas ages 5   Like
           Evans

Animls

My favourite animl is a rabbit. it wos a late Birthday Present. Her name is Bunty. I Love her lots. She is white with Brown spots. Bunty has a squashed nose Which makes me laugh. she Plays ball with me.

BY KATHRYN ROSS
Age 8

Animals

My pet hamster is called Flufey, she goes to sleep in the Morning.
But at night she is Noisey when she goes in her wheel, that is
when she is Noisey. Wakes me up at Night. In the Morning when I
feed her she Some times bites Me. Not often.

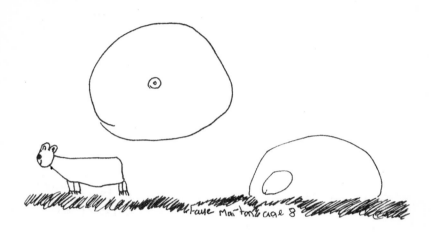

Faye Marton age 8

Animals

Down the beach,
On a dusty donkey,
At the zoo,
Looking at a monkey.

I had a rabbit,
With ears so floppy,
We had a dalmatian,
He was also dotty.

In the sea,
A big dark whale,
Oh just look at that,
A puppy dog's tail.

By Charlotte Sewart.
Age 10.

Friday 25th april 1997

(JADSO) X
Jason Parker

age 9

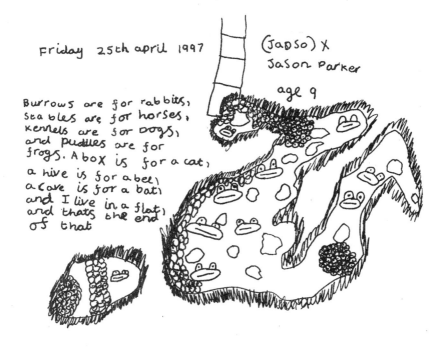

Burrows are for rabbits,
stables are for horses,
kennels are for dogs,
and puddles are for
frogs. A box is for a cat,
a hive is for a bee,
a cave is for a bat,
and I live in a flat,
and thats the end
of that

Animals

Foxes with long,
Orange tails.
Big, Black,
  Killer whales.

Brown, White
And Spotty dogs,
Small Spikey,
Brown Hedgehog.

Big Lions with
Orange manes,
Black and White
Pandas with Bamboo canes

Baby Bunnies
In Burrows they dig
And at last my favourite
A small pink pig!

By Madeleine Webb
Age: 10.

Little Spotty Doggy

Little Spotty Dotty Doggy
feeling rather Grotty.
Eat Something funny that
Up-Set his tummy.
Running home much faster,
to his master.

Joanne Eve Upton. Age -8

maisie

My favourite animal is a dog and I
Love him.

Age 4. Name: Maisie Ellis

Animals

I have three rabbits called
Polo, Rolo and Tolo. Polo is the
oldest, Rolo is in between and
Tolo is the youngest.
Polo is a Netherland Dwarf whilst
Rolo and Tolo are dutch rabbits.
I also have a hamster who has a
birthday on the same day as me.
I have ten goldfish as well.
Then I would like a horse or a dog.
All my pets mean a lot to me.

by Claire Dignan Age: 10

Animals

I love animals, especially cats and wild cats. I
love all animals. I love kittens.

Poem

I love animals, I love cats
    I love kittens
    I love tigers

I love Lions I love every
    animal in the
        world

by Daisy pattison

Age 9

Animals.

My pets are all very special to me.
My dog Poppy, My bird Joe and my
two large Goldfish Grant and Phil.
I also have an angry hamster called Mini.

by Matthew Woolley
Age 11

My cat is called Dennis. He is a fuffy cat
I Love Dennis

SALLy ANNe neal Age 6

My Dog Mac.

My dog Mac is covered in fleas.
She scratches and scratches but they still tease.
Sometimes she lies flat on her belly and
She sleep's with her head in my tatty old welly

By Lucy Hudson
Age 11

My favorite animal is a bat. My favorite bat is a long-eared-bat.
I like bats because most pepole hate bats and because they hunt
by echo-location. I also like bats because thair are lots of diffrent
sorts of bats. I also like bats because they come out at night
                                                    Nick sadler
                                                    age 7

Animals

One morning I woke and my mum said that we were going to the Zoo. When I got up
I got dressed, had my breakfast, got in the car and we were off. On the way
me and my family were talking about the Zoo. When we got there we went to pay and
get the food and drinks for animals to have. There were lots of different animals,
not just Zoo animals. First we went to the Lions. We had to be really careful
incase they bit us. My dad said he would feed them. We didn't need to give the Lions
a drink. Then we went to the guinea pigs. I love guinea pigs because I've got two.
The guinea pigs only needed a drink so mum said I could do it.

                                    age 8   Lisa Seaton

Nature

Nature is all the creatures around us. We Should look after
nature. It Will look after us. We Should help nature, and
Nature will help us. I Like nature. Nature is allsorts
of creepy crawlies. Nature is nice and beautifull.
And Sometimes colourful.

                    by Kirsty Sharp age 8year

Animals

My rabbit is called Smokey. One day my friend called Kathy came to my house. I said to her, "do you want to come and see my new rabbit?" "Yes I will because I haven't seen one in ages." So I took her into the back garden. I said "you can take her out of the hutch if you like". Then I just went to get some carrots and I saw her running round the garden. Kathy said, "I opened the cage, and she just jumped out". It was about a hour before we caught her.

The End

by Emily Rushton Age 9

Friday 25th April 1997

Stables are for horses,
Kennels are for dogs,
Burrows are for rabbits
and puddles are for frogs.
a web is for a spider,
a box is for a cat,
a hive is for a bee
and a cave is for a bat.
a sty is for a pig,
a hole is for a mouse,
a nest is for a bird,
but I live in a house

copied by Lewis Rook.

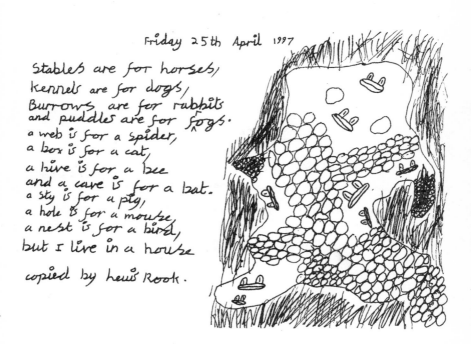

TIGER

Tiger tiger running fast,
Chasing zebra through the grass.
Tiger kills so he can eat,
No man eats the tiger meat.

Tiger tiger on the run,
Running from the hunter's gun.
Hunted for his skin and bones,
Hear the tiger's mournful groans.

Tiger's blood is on the blade,
Now no zebra are afraid.
The world is less. You are gone.
Humans your fur coat put on.

Paul Chaplin

I lik anl maemals

JodYMartln
age6

Horses

Horses, foals everywhere
Looking after their foals with
care.
Galloping round and round and
round making lots and lots of
sound.
Out for a ride when the foals
hide.
Time for bed for a tired Ned.

By Amie Cunningham 8½

Animals
I love animals because they are
cute. I love dogs. They are very,
very, very cute and soft and cuddly.
I love zoo animals as well, my favourite
animal is a monkey.

By Shaun Sheldon
Age 8

Animals

My favourite animal is a cat. I have three called Sweep Narla and Simba. One is ginger. one is white and black. While the last one is all black.

Narla and Simba knock over litter bins and roll on the floor, but Sweep does not.

by Jenny Whitbread

I am 8

---

my brothers cat was bitten by the dog. Her jaw was broken and her nose was bleeding. we hav to mash her food up. She is a bit better now.

Heather Archer. Age 7

Animals.

I have a dog which I really adore. He likes to eat. Pedigree Chum. It is not meat it is biscuits but he will not eat it if it has not got any of our food in. His name is George. mum and I take him for long walks every day. He likes to jump up at me when he sees me after School. I like to give him cuddles.

By clare walker age 7.

Hobbies

Walkers

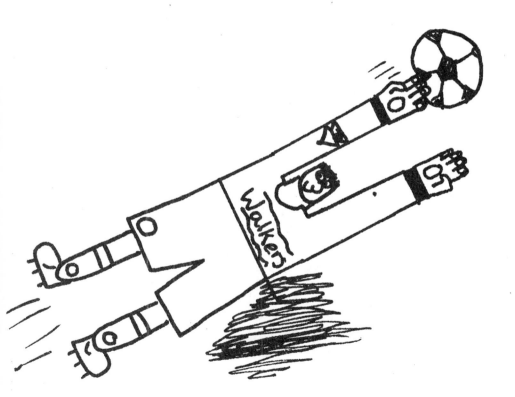

Hobbies

My favourite hobbies are dancing, swimming, fencing and gymnastics. My favourite hobby is dancing. I do it 4 days a week. I do tap, ballet, modern, acro, solos and groups. I am having a new song and dance. When I grow up I want to be in the Olympics. I might win a medal, I hope I do. On wednesday I play tennis with school. I enjoy doing tennis. I have 14 pets: 1 dog, 1 cat, 4 newts, 5 fish, 2 stickleback and 1 crab.

Raychel Conway
Age 8

Hobbies

My Hobby is football.
I play on right wing.
I've scored ten goals this season.
Thats quite a good thing.
Our managers Mick Ballard.
He's helped us alot.
Without him we'd soon drop.
From weak to week we're going down.
Without Mick Ballard we may as well go home and sit down.

By Jean Betts
Age 9

Hobbies

My hobby is football
My hobby is pool
My hobby is basketball.
My hobbies grow tall
I'm not too keen on cricket, I can't
hit the wicket.
But football fills me with delight, I dream
about it every night. By Jonathan Fines
Age. 9 .

Wen i FLY my kit
iT maks me hapey

Bes iT maks my mum

giv me a LoLey

Daniel Lockwood

age b

Hobbies.

H. is for hobbies, mine is football.

O. is for one I've scored this season.

b. is for bored when I'm on the sideline.

b. is for boot, I blast the ball with.

I. is for I hope because I hope I'll play when I'm older.

E. is for easy tackling people.

S. is for sunday when we play.

by Tom Hammond age 9.

I like duwing my shows
bcus I like the dansing
and my danses

I like my acrow best
bcus F like bore feet
and it is an indyun dans
melissa warren
age 6

Hobbies

My hobbies are Football and art. I'm really good at art. Art is my best out the both of them, I'm good at football too. My favourite position is goalie because I can do brilliant saves.

Dane Burton
Age 9

hobis. I Like Playing With my dog. I Like Playing On the computer. Some days I don't Like Playing.

Jordan Golding age 7

Hobbies

I bowled an extra fast Yorker,
It hit a boy called Porker,
It sent him into outer space
And now my cricket is a disgrace!

Peter Roberts
10 years old

My favourite hobby is making things because I like geting messy and geting sticky hands. I make a mess all over the plase. When iam finished I am really proud of myself.

Adam clarkson Age 7

My Hobbies

I like P.E. because we can do athletics and we can do cricket and sometimes we can do football and long jump. We do running races and we do tennis.

Ian Merryweather
Age 8

Hobbies.

My favourite hobbies are swimming, dancing and music. I play the recorder and the keyboard. I do a bit of dancing too. I do acrobatics and madern. My favourite hobby is swimming. I swim for Loughborough Town Swimming Club. I swim with Samantha and Anna. They are my best friends,

By Jay Bunyan.
Age 10.

I like playing Football because I want to be good at it. I like playing on my cumputer. I got it yesterday. I like playing on my bike. And I like going very Fast. I like playing with my Toys. I like going out places. I Like helping my Daddy warter the plants.

Robert Palmer. 7

My favourite hobby is football. My secund favourlte is basKiTball becos I am goodatit. I am fast. I play golf. Som times I get a hol in one. My hobbies Keep me busy

Thomas Sturgess

age7

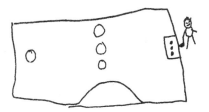

Hobbies

My favourite sport is Formula One Motot Racing. This is one of the most glamorous sports in the world. Every race is called a Grand Prix. Of course I have never raced but I have sat in a Formula One car. I support Damon Hill who races for T.W.R. Arrows-Honda. My favourite Circuit is Hokkinen and one day I would like to visit it

BY Thomas North
Age 10

WEN I LIVd in AMarica I PLayd fotba-L in 2 tems

Jack prince
age 6

My Hobbies

My Hobbies are Football and swimming. I play Football on Tuesday and Sunday. I like football the best I play for Barrow Juniors under11s team. Our team clours are red and black I am a midfielder which I enjoy because I get to do everthing. I like swimming because it is great fun I go swimming on saturday.

by Ben McDonagh

Age 11.

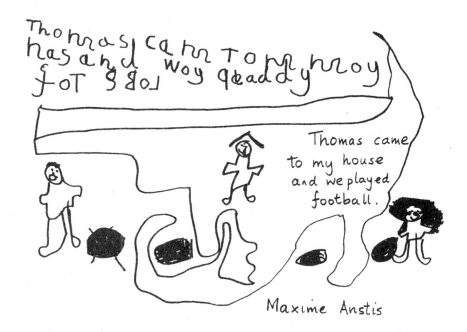

Thomas came to my house and we played football.

Maxime Anstis

Hobbies

My hobbies are football, cricket and Tennis. I like football because I am good at it. I like cricket because I can bowl people out easily. Tennis is my favourite hobby.

By Ben Pollard
Aged 9.

My favourite eom is play on my key bod.

my favourite game is playing on my keyboard

Emily Golder

Hobbies

I am on the way to the swimming pool.
This is my first race . I walk into the changing rooms
and get changed.
I am on the starting block .
I know I am going to win this race.
The man shouts "go."
25 metres to go and I am still in second place.
5 metres to go and I am level ,
the last metre I just reach out and.......... "YES!"
I won.

By Ben Fairbrother
Age 10

Hobbies.

I do swimming 3 times a week, Monday, Thursday and Saturday. I might start on a Sunday. I did some races the other day and I came 1st, 2nd, 3rd and 4th. I also play the recorder, guitar and I play the keyboard at home. I also do dancing, I used to do ballet and now I do modern. I do acrobatics and I can do the splits. We also looked at a notice about line-dancing, which I might start.

Anna Norris
Age 10

Hobbies.

Hobbies, hobbies, hobbies.
Everybody has them. Even I do. I like pool, snooker, football and stamp collecting. My favourite is football. I play mostly at lunch on the field or the playground but I've only ever scored three times. I think that your personality is involved around your hobbies, so looking at my hobbies I'm pretty cool.

Robbie Lewis.

My Hobbies

My Hobbies are swimming and football. I like football the best because I play more of it. Our team colours are red and black, I play in midfield.
I also play tennis I have won a lot of trophies.

by Charles Mauger age 10

mummyBDaDgKayleigh
leigh
and me at f b

Mummy, Daddy,
Kayleigh, Leigh and me
at football.

Richard Gray

<u>Hobbies</u>

My hobby is Cricket.
You've got to hit the wicket.
IF you can't hit the wicket,
then don't bother playing Cricket.

Craig Smith
10 years old

I have a football sticker of Ian Wright He plays for Aresenal and he's my my all time hero. Sometimes I sit and look at this sticker and dream. Will I ever play for a premiership club? Oh well, I'm happy playing for Barrow.

Colin Ross age 11

MY HOBBIES

My favourite hobby is football and I support Liverpool football club. When I am older I want to be just like Robbie Fowler and play for Liverpool.
  I also like playing pool and snooker .
My dad thinks I am superb because I beat him every time.

Iain Ross
Age 11

Hobbies.
I love horses every day,
I would cry if they ran away,
Up and down, over the Jump,
And landing with a heavy thump,
Brushing here, brushing there
Just look at all that horse's hair.

By Amy Whitmore
Age:9

my favourite game
is racing cars in
the arcade.

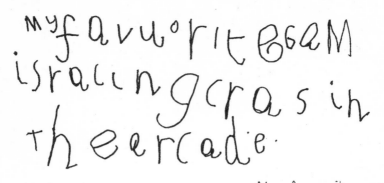

My favourite game
is racing cars in the
arcade

Danny Henson

Hobbies
swimming is my favourite
hobby. I like it because
I enjoy jumping in the pool.
Already I have gained my
passin badge, 5 metre/10 metre
and pull frog three.
my favourite stroke is frog
legs and I can dive to the
bottom as the pool and do
a somersalt. After this
I do a handstand in the water.

peter conway
age 7.

I wish I was a football player
for mahehslter Uhited.
My favourite Player is Cantona.
He is the best!

By Jason cory

Age 7.

My Hobbies

My hobbies are dancing. I go to Ballet
and Tap on Wednesday and modern
dancing on a Friday. I also like running
and swimming. I like playing rounders
and netball too. My life is very busy
but I would not have it any other way.

By Laura Morris.
age 10

Hobbies

I Love Singing. I hope to be on
Top of the Pops and be at number one
and see the Spice girls and
Ant and Dec and other groups.
It would be great to be famous on

teley

keith wiDDowson
age 8 years old.

My favourite
racing cars

Thomas Needham

Hobbies

My favourite hobby is swimming. I am really good and
fast at backstroke, I have passed my bronze and
my silver awards. I have also gained my 1000 metre
badge.
Another of my hobbies is making up exciting stories.
and colouring in lots of pictures really nicely.
I also enjoy handling animals and admiring dolphins.
I would just love to ride on a dolphin.

By Jennifer Roberts.
age 8.

L.T.

My favourite sport is swimming. I swim for Loughborough swimming club. My favourite stroke is breststroke. My sister, swims for Loughborough too. This is what I sing at a gala "1.2.3.4. who are we going to shout for? Not the King not the queen but the Loughborough team." My best times are freestyle 20.63 breast 24.23 fly 32.89 back 23.64. By christopher Bunyan age 8

My Hobbies

Friday night is my favourite night, because I go to
football training.
Sam comes with me and we have a great time .
I support Leicester city and my hero is Steve Walsh .
I even got a signed photogragh .
One day when I am old , I would like to play for Leicester city
too. But guess what I am a GIRL!

By Kelly Tilley
Age 11

Hobbies

I woke up. I wished I could be better than Michael Jordan. He is very, very, very good at basket ball . I want to meet all of the characters of the cartoon. We would have a match and we would only win by one point.
Nathan Hort
Age 7

I bic pley wic Lauren
sum sots Tis wiy play

I like playing
with Lauren. Sometimes
we play 'stars'.

Jayne Reilly

Hobbies

My hobby is Dancing. I do Acro, Tap
and ballet. I think I'm good at acro.
I do Tap on Monday and I do Acro
and ballet on wednesday. Anaysian
and Lisa go too. My sister goes on Friday aswell.
on Thursday I go and help. I go at Quorn.
on Thursday its at the church rooms.
Its fantastic!
by Hannah Johnston
age 8

I really like playing the violin because it makes me feel very happy. I really enjoy it. My teacher Mrs. Cunningham is really encouraging. Lately I took my Grade one exam and passed with a merit of 127. I am taking my Grade two next year.

by
Rachel Webster.
age 10

I LIKE PLAYing FOOt ball becg it mach your Legs sthong. And I LIKe runn ing becus it macs your Legs sthong. And I LIKe PLAYing snooker.

michael Dut.
Age 7.

Hobbies

My Hobbies are football, basketball, computers, running, snooker, swimming, and skateboarding. Football is my favourite. I play in defence for Barrow Rangers and i go football training every Friday. I support Manchester United.

by Paul morris age 9
year 4

my zavourite gam
ezmygraðecatg

my favourite game
is 'fraidy cats'.

Koren McCallum·Thake

Hobby.

My favourite hobby is cricket because
I am good at cricket and I play a
lot of cricket every day. My dad teaches
me how to catch and my dad taught me
how to bat and bowl and field too. I play
for a team. cricket makes me feel happy
when I play.

Sunshine warne.
age : 7 years old.

My Hobbies

I like football, rounders and cricket. I play them in my spare time. My favourite sport is long jump, but we do that at school in games. Sport is fantastic, as it brings everybody together. Even my baby sister and brother will play with me then.

By
Samantha
Dearlove
Age 10

Hobbies

My hobby is collecting toy monkeys. I have alot at home. I have a favourite one. It is a smallish one and I had it for my first Easter. My favourite one is a boy called Moco. My most unusual one is purple with a yellow face.

by Jacqui Thorpe

Aged 8

My Hobbies

My hobbies are playing with my dog, playing on the computer and going fishing. When I say " tig tig cats!" my dog chases my friends and me. I play on my computer and beat my brother. Sometimes I go fishing with my brother or friends, and I have been to the sea catching fish. I caught two eels and a different fish that I've forgotten the name of!

By Peter Mitton
Age 11

Hobbies

I play football in my back garden. I play football with my friends. I watch football on the television. I support Manchester United. My other hobby is computers. I play on my computer at home. I've got a pc at home. I have got a game called lemmings and I've got pool and chess and drafts on my computer. I play on a Game Boy. Game boys are cool. I've got loads of games with it. I've got a skateboard at home and I like playing on my skateboard.

By Andrew perry   Age 9
year 4

William

This is me
playing
football.

Age 4. Name: William Foster

Hobbies

I am a fan of Damon Hill. He is a Formula one racing driver, he races for TWR Arrows - Yamaha and he is reigning world champion. My favourite racing circuit is Monaco. Every race is called a Grand Prix and is held every two or three weeks. I would really like to go and see the Monaco Grand Prix.

By Neil Brightman
Age 10

Hobbies

I love to run and swim. Running is good because you can get lots of medals. Swimming is good too because you can help someone and get life-saving badges. I like running the best especially when you run against other schools — that is the best of all.

By Hannah Joyce (age 9)

Hobbies

my hobbies are football. I want to be a football player when I am older. I want to play for Leicester City and I want to play mid field. I have been to watch five Leicester matches. They have won one and drawn 4. my dad and my cousin went to some of the games and my next door neighbour.

Joseph wilson   age 9

ILIC wooch l9 v LdoS

I like watching videos.

Richard Betts

age 5

Days out

I Love my Bike rides Because I can change my

gears . and it can go paster . I broonar like hute we can play

hide and seak in the Balls. we went on noredny

to prance. we played poot Ball in the

Feardes.

Chure
Chare

Misercigy
Blaise pollard
age 7

I have many different hobbies. My favourite is Swimming. At the moment I am working on my Gold Award. My other hobbies are Guides on Mondays, Running club on Thursdays and football on Fridays. And I enjoy them All.

by Samantha Lockwood.

Age 10

I like futbul and swiming and runingandriding my bic I likeswiming underwutrandtobi tehis.

Alex Harris.
Age 7.

Hobbies

My hobby is horse riding.
I do trotting and cantering.

I like horse jumping.
We do twenty metre circles.
Sometimes we go on a hack.

Christopher Robson age9

I l c c a r s

I like cars

James Dul age 5

my hobbies are riding Acrobatics and Football.

I like riding because I like ponies and because it's good fun I like Acerbatics because I ysed to go every week and I like football because I play it with my dad evry nite.

Katie Halliwell Age 6

Hobby

My hobby is racing real mini cars.
It is very good, fast, scary and
exciting. There is alot of hard work
but it's fun.
We have one mini it is red and it
has the number 101 on it's doors.
   My first race takes place in two
weeks time. I am feeling just a bit
nervous.

        Lee robinson
            Age 10

My hobbie's are Dancing and riding. The reason I like Dancing is
because I am bendy Well infact very bendy indeed and because
My sister goe's as well. Last but not lest the reason I like
riding is because I like Pony's. My fafrit pony is Poly because she
bose what I say.

            Sophie Etchells
            Age 7

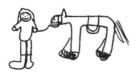

Hobbies

My favourite hobby is football. Sometimes I like running. I like
footy because I enjoy playing It. I like tennis as well.

Jonathan Mckay
Age 9

Hobbies

I love playing football it is my favourite
sport and I also like playing cricket.
When I am older I want to play
football for England in a world Cup Final.
But I do not think I will. At the moment
I play for Barrow Juniors. We are third in
our League. We reached the quarter final of
the League Cup. It was a really close
game. Even though we lost, it has not put
me off football.

Richard Barkby   Age 11

Feelings

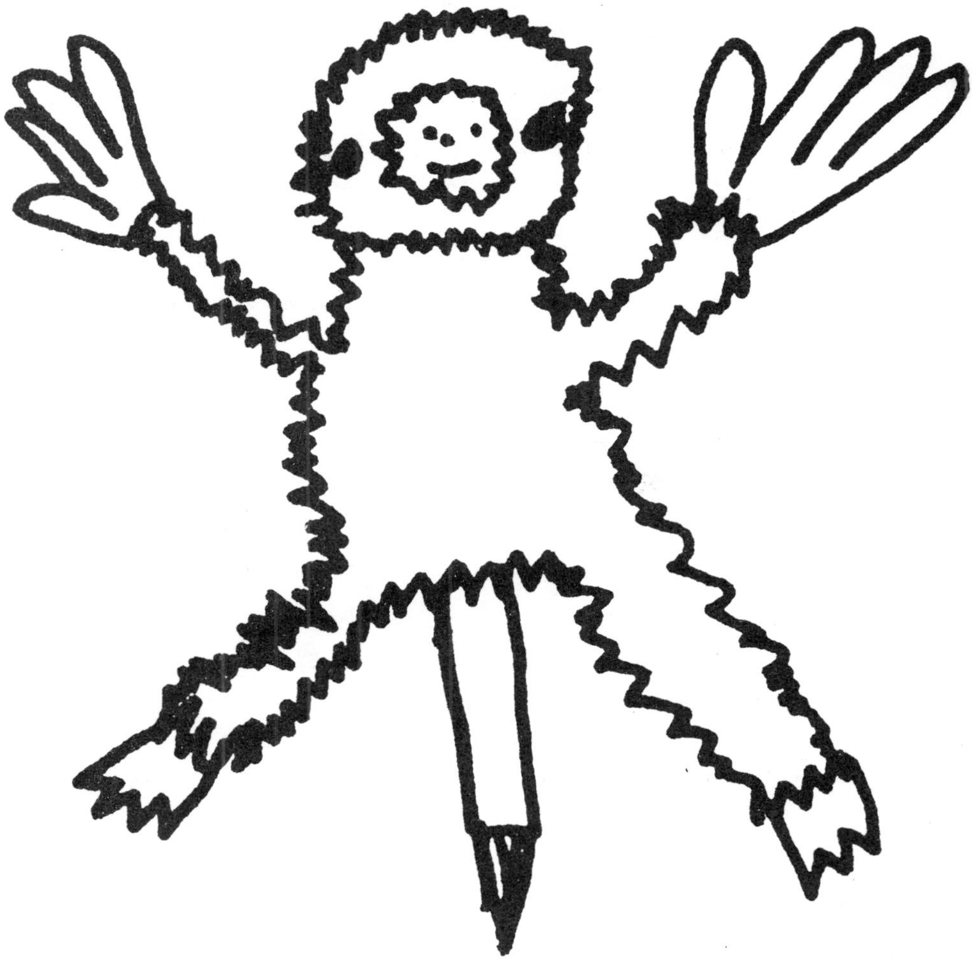

Feelings

Feelings, feelings everywhere.
Happy, Sad, to love and care.
Hatred, guilt and unfair,
Sometimes angry to lie and scare.

Feelings, feelings all day long.
Can be heard in word or Song.
Sympathy when things go wrong.
Feelings, feelings right or wrong.

Feelings, feelings in the night,
Sensitive, Happiness to dream kill light.
Envy, anger, all through the night,
So make nice feelings until light.

Colette Laxton
10 years

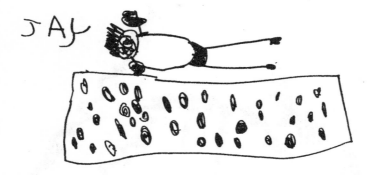

I feel happy when I go swimming.

Age 4. Name: Jay Elphick

I feel hapey because Sum won Scored for Lester
So they Wun the coca cola cup. I feel Sad because my
rabit died and my dog died as well. I feel hapey because
I can do the monkey bars all the way across. I feel Sad
because my grandad died.
go to the park.
I feel hapey because I can

Age Nicholas Lockwood

SnOWY
MaKes
me HAPpy

XXX

Samuel Thorpe Age 5

My Jumper

My Jumper is not a cricket jumper,
but my friend says it is.
Please do not believe him
as he has got a zebra sweatshirt.

By Lee Hodgess
Age 11

I feel   happy
becus I go to
chriss and swess
haws.

Brett Shw Age 6

My Feelings.
From Reception to today,
Now soon I'll be on my way.
Now in Year six I'm in a fix,
For all the years I've been through,
I'm going to miss all of you.

By Richard Shaw
age 11

I Licepae the peel

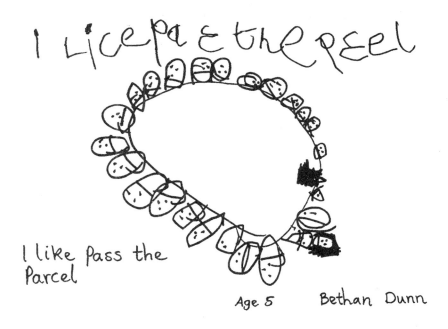

I like pass the Parcel

Age 5   Bethan Dunn

I feel happy when King takes me quod bikeing. I feel excixed when I ride my bike. I feel sad when I fall over. I felt suprised when mummy piked me up and there was a big dog in the car.

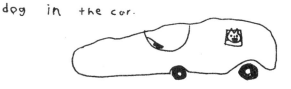

Joshua Rundle Age 7

I am Happy when LEICESTER win and sad when I
fall over When I get excited it feels good. When I am
frigntened I go to my friends I feel Happy I am glad that
most of the time I feel Happy.

Luke Hickling
Age 7

I felt Sad wh I
wS PLY

I felt sad when I was poorly.

Ben Golder

I feel happy wen I'm at the
fair. The rids are fun.
yOU can have hot dogs.
Gemma charlesworth.
Age 6.

Feelings of . . . .

Disappointment.
Happiness.
Sadness.
Anger.
Jealousy.
Hate.
Love.
Betrayel.
Romance.
Fear.
Excitement.
How have you felt today? Aimee Grewcock 9 years

Humphrey macs
me Happy

Age 5   Jessica Acton

I am sad when my Dad shouts at me and when my Sister gets things. I am Sad When I cant go to macdonalds and when I cant go out at Play time.

David Alexander.
Age 7.

When I was young I felt I could turn nowhere.
I had no friends at all, I was sad and lonely.
I sat in the playground watching everyone play.
Wondering if anyone would come and ask me,
But they never did.
    Now I am older I feel I can go anywhere.
I have many friends and I feel happy and wanted.
I play in the playground and join in with the games.
Who needs asking? I am one of the group.
Ready to take on the world!

by Amy Hough.
age 11.

I feel happy when my mum givs my some sweets.

darren Sutton   age 7

I felt happy when I went to the zoo and the monkys kisst my monky throw the window. Evrybody was crowding around us. It was very very Exsiting.

Jane Middleton. Age 7.

My family make me feel happy.

Age 4. Name: Scott Pestell

Daniel

When I go swimming
I feel happy.

Age 4. Name: Daniel Higgins

Sometimes I feel like the lost sheep,
stuck on a little ledge, so that if I
even try to turn round, I would fall off.
I am going nowhere. My wool is torn
and ragged and it is very, very cold so
I cannot feel anything. All my friends
have gone away and I am on my
own. They seem happy enough, but I
am scared. Sometimes I cannot even
see them. When will my shepherd come
and find me? Sometimes, I think he will
never come.

by Danielle Smith aged 11.